W9-AUM-093

Katreena

Finding Sarah

2012

Dear Katreena

love

Sarah

The Duchess

of York.

ALSO BY SARAH FERGUSON

Victoria and Albert—Life at Osborne House
Travels with Queen Victoria
My Story
Dining with the Duchess
Dieting with the Duchess
Win the Weight Game
Reinventing Yourself with the Duchess of York
Energy Breakthrough
What I Know Now
Moments

Books for Younger Readers

Budgie the Little Helicopter
Budgie at Bendick's Point
Budgie and the Blizzard
The Adventures of Budgie
Budgie Goes to Sea
Budgie's Book of Colors
Budgie and Pippa Count to Ten!
The Royal Switch
Bright Lights
Little Red
Little Red's Christmas Story

Little Red's Autumn Adventure
Little Red's Summer Adventure
Little Red to the Rescue
Tea for Ruby

The Helping Hand Series:

Ashley Learns About Strangers
Jacob Goes to the Doctor
Michael and His New Baby Brother
Emily's First Day at School
When Katie's Parents Separated
Matthew and the Bullies
Olivia Says Goodbye to Grandpa
Molly Makes Friends
Harry Starts to Enjoy His Food
Simon Gets Better
Jack Takes More Exercise

Finding Sarah

A DUCHESS'S JOURNEY

TO FIND HERSELF

Sarah Ferguson

The Duchess of York

ATRIA BOOKS

New York • London • Toronto • Sydney

ATRIA BOOKS

A Division of Simon & Schuster, Inc.
1230 Avenue of the Americas
New York, NY 10020

Copyright © 2011 by Sarah Ferguson, The Duchess of York

All rights reserved, including the right to reproduce this book or
portions thereof in any form whatsoever. For information,
address Atria Books Subsidiary Rights Department,
1230 Avenue of the Americas, New York, NY 10020.

Permissions for photographs and previously published material
used in this book are listed after the Acknowledgments.

First Atria Books hardcover edition June 2011

ATRIA BOOKS and colophon are trademarks of Simon & Schuster, Inc.

For information about special discounts for bulk purchases,
please contact Simon & Schuster Special Sales at
1-866-506-1949 or business@simonandschuster.com.

The Simon & Schuster Speakers Bureau can bring authors to your live event.
For more information or to book an event, contact the Simon & Schuster Speakers
Bureau at 1-866-248-3049 or visit our website at www.simonspeakers.com.

Designed by Dana Sloan

Manufactured in the United States of America

10 9 8 7 6 5 4 3 2 1

ISBN 978-1-4391-8954-2
ISBN 978-1-4391-8956-6 (ebook)

This book is dedicated
to Oprah who pulled
me out of the darkness,
and my dearest Andrew
who holds onto the
Real Sarah and of
Course, with all my
heart and soul to
my Magical 2 Beautiful
daughters, Beatrice and
Eugenie who remain
true and steadfast to
their Mummy.

Contents

My Dear Reader   xi

1. | Lost   1

2. | Journey   17

3. | The Lotus Flower   41

4. | Far from the Madding Crowd   47

5. | Montecito   51

6. | Lifeline   61

7. | Return to Dummer   69

8. | Sister Act   75

9. | Looking for Love   83

10. | Mind Chatter   89

11. | The People-Pleaser   103

12. | The Two Wolves   109

13. | I Swallowed a Duvet   113

14.	The Miracle Man	125
15.	"I Am a Thousand Winds That Blow"	135
16.	No-Man's-Land	147
17.	Healing in the Desert	155
18.	Into the Maze	165
19.	Heather Blaze	175
20.	Horse Power	183
21.	Bent but Not Broken	197
22.	No Mission Impossible	211
23.	Rejuvenation	221
24.	Wedding Bells	231
25.	Adventure as Therapy	245
26.	The Great Slave Lake	255
27.	Kamalaya	265
28.	Mr. Carpenter	277
29.	The Ant and the Buzzing Bee	283
30.	Breakthrough	289
31.	Hugging Pain	297
32.	Found	301
	Acknowledgments	309

S

My dear reader,

"To love one's self is the beginning of a lifelong romance."

—OSCAR WILDE

More than a year ago, my life was so off course that I wondered whether I would ever be able to find my way back. I was in the gutter, no question. I had suffered the consequences of a bad decision, made without careful reasoning. I had flung myself into a mess, unthinkingly, like someone who dives into a pool without checking the depth. I found myself walking around asking why I was even living. I was broken and lost, not even sure where I was, but out of this emotional barrenness I knew I had to find me. *And so, I took a journey to find myself and begin the process of healing all the broken places.* Finding Sarah *is the story of that journey.*

There is a reason I have chosen to share my journey with you. There was a time in my life when I would have been paralyzed by the adversity I've experienced. But I have come to understand that a terrible experience, though difficult at the time, can become a source of strength and courage.

While it is my journey, it is also yours. I honestly believe that if you and I were to sit down together, it is likely we would discover more things that we have in common than things which set us apart. In listening to my story, you might say, "Oh, that feels like what I've been through."

So many of us, though we may not admit it, have lost ourselves at one point or another—whether through divorce, loss of a loved one, addiction, illness, depression, or some other life trauma. And somehow, some way, we must find our way back. It is never too late to find a new direction, realize a dream, or take back control of your life.

On any journey, there are people you meet who enrich your experience more than the places you visit. I had amazing guides—real-life angels—who shined the light on the dark parts of my life and helped me find my way back. I met them during the taping of my docu-series, Finding Sarah, *and you will meet them on every page of this book and learn from them, as I did. They are experts who helped me understand the source of all my problems—from comfort eating to self-loathing, from reckless overspending to the notorious mishaps I habitually find myself in. But there are other guides, too—my friends and family who offered me support and wisdom along the way, and I include bits of their guiding wisdom on these pages as well. I believe that some of the most loving, wise advice comes from those who know us well, and love us even more.*

Finding Sarah *is not a self-help book in the traditional sense. Nor is it a how-to program with steps. Rather, it is my attempt to inspire you, through my own experiences, to think about how nagging aspects of your own life may be holding you back, then to encourage you to follow your instincts and find your true path.*

As it turned out, *Finding Sarah* segmented naturally into thirty-two parts. Significantly, the number 32 in many spiritual practices represents truth and how to live it. Finding the truth of who I am is at the heart of my journey.

As I wrote this book, both who I am and where I've been became clearer to me, more defined. I have seen where my life took wrong turns. I can point to places where I changed, the events and people who taught me the meaning of joy, and the steep hills where I felt the burden of despair.

When our lives are in harmony, we have an instinctive sense of the right direction. We can move steadily ahead through life without fear of getting lost, knowing that through the storms and uncertainties, we shall come to the right place at last.

My hope and prayer is that you will find that "Right Place" in your own life, as I am beginning to—life is a work in progress.

love Sarah,

Finding Sarah

1 | *Lost*

I can't believe I created such a merry hell.

ℴNCE UPON A time I was a princess, married to a handsome prince, and living in a palace. But then the fairy tale began to unravel. I got divorced, started my life over with two young daughters, went broke twice, and watched my life be brutally sensationalized by the international press. I never imagined I could live so unhappily ever after.

As I write this, I am immersed in extreme personal turbulence, and I am trying to buckle up with whatever remains in my emotional and spiritual resources. The facts are these: In May 2010, my life spiraled into a private hell when I was caught unawares, on a hidden camera, accepting money from a tabloid reporter posing as an Indian business tycoon who supposedly wanted to back my various business ventures.

The whole mess started innocently enough, when I began looking for investors willing to put their capital in my business and help me rebuild a loyal following for my books, merchandising, and other enterprises. One of these projects was to build a girls' school in Afghanistan.

Any business that needs investors or financing is usually required to produce a business plan—showing information such as financial reports, projections, and the company's goals before receiving funding. I had a business plan—a strong one. Even so, my business had suffered in recent years because so much money had been taken up with paying wages and past bills. A repercussion of this mess was my inability to pay the wages of a longtime friend and trusted staff member. He needed that money to pay for his college tuition and room and board—to the tune of forty thousand US dollars. I wanted to help him.

In my own defense, I have always been a great one for giving. I played Santa all year round. I never saw my generosity as a fault. I got such a high from showing friends what I thought of them; it was almost addictive with me. I craved the appreciation and approval that came from pleasing other people. It was always about buying everyone's affection. I had to be the best fun, the most generous, because obviously no one could like Sarah for who she really was.

As for keeping my businesses alive, I had no idea how I would come up with the money, since at the time I was seriously about to go bankrupt.

Financial rescue seemed in sight when my friend—the person who could not make his college expenses—and I learned that a mutual friend of ours could introduce me to an investor who would help me. The mutual friend told us that this individual was a successful, well-known businessman from India who worked for a prestigious conglomerate of companies and that he wanted to back my projects.

And indeed, when we checked, there was such a company that did have this person working for them. He was legitimate—he came highly referenced—and by all accounts, he was for real. Optimistic, I agreed to the introduction.

From that point forward, everything was set in motion, irrevocably so. I first met with this businessman at the Mark Hotel in New York City. I asked him to sign a confidentiality agreement, to which he agreed, and he would sign at the next meeting.

Several days later, I asked two of my assistants to retrieve the signed agreement. He had not signed it, however. He curled it up, and said, "I just need to give it to my lawyers."

I smelled a powerful, foul odor that best can be described as dead rats in the basement. My instincts told me not to do it, that it wasn't right, that I couldn't trust him. Despite twinges of something amiss, I said to myself, "No," because this agreement would mean I'd be able to meet my needs and take care of all the people who were important to me. I recklessly plowed forward.

Back in London, I texted the businessman to have dinner with me at Mosimann's, a fancy wood-paneled restaurant in the shape of an octagon. Ironically, the building was once a nineteenth-century church, a place originally intended for peace and spiritual refuge.

When I arrived, I asked him if he had signed the confidentiality agreement. He said, "I'll do it tomorrow morning." I felt he might be waffling, but I went on with dinner anyway.

Over a meal of pea soup, a main course of lamb and vegetables, and a bottle of Burgundy, we discussed how our business venture would play out. After we finished eating, the man paid our dinner tab. I jumped into a limousine with him to travel to what he claimed was his flat in the trendy Mayfair district of London.

During our meeting, I mentioned in passing that by doing business with me, he might get to meet Prince Andrew, because the Prince and I are a team. Under no circumstances did I offer to broker an introduction to my former husband, as it has been claimed. I love Andrew to this day, as I did when I met and married him, and I would never, ever, sell him out or betray him.

Of course, the British press and international media spun the truth into a web of lies. On the now infamous, surreptitious videotape that has been broadcast around the world, you see me making a rather sloppy spectacle of myself, sipping too much wine and puffing on a cigarette. The tape was purposely cut to look like I was brokering a personal introduction. Which, as I have said, I did not do. It was edited, completely out of context, and showed the following conversation:

"Is that a deal?" he asked.

"Yes," and I shook his hand, staring straight into his eyes. "Look after me, and he'll look after you."

The full sum would "open up everything," I told him.

"I don't want to get anybody in trouble or just . . ." he said.

"But you will be his friend."

"Great. But his job is trade, isn't it? Isn't it his job?"

"Yes, it is, but he meets the most amazing people."

"Well, let's do it."

"He never does accept a penny for anything."

"No, of course not, no."

The investor produced wads of cash from a safe—forty thousand dollars—and dropped the bills down in front of me on the coffee table. Those funds represented a good-faith down payment. The other investment money would be wired to my bank account. He handed me the money in a black computer bag, and I got in my car to be taken home by my driver, Harry.

Honestly, I was elated over the business arrangement. It was all very heady and wonderful. I wanted to believe that this man would put his money to work for me, I really did.

The next day, my daughter Beatrice and I took the train up to Newcastle University to see my other daughter, Eugenie, who is a student there. We had a lovely picnic together. I was in such a great mood, relieved to be away from negativity, snuggled safely away from the pressures of everyday life.

A huge proud moment came for me that week on May 20 when Beatrice, Eugenie, and I unveiled the Teenage Cancer Trust unit at the Great North Children's Hospital in Newcastle, a stone's throw from where Eugenie was studying.

I have lost friends to cancer—my father, stepfather, best friend, and grandfather. They all succumbed to this dreaded disease—and I have had scares myself, too, so this charity holds a particular place in my heart.

I have been a royal patron of the Teenage Cancer Trust for more than twenty years. Its mission is to build specialist units so that youngsters do not have to go through the frightening experience of being treated on an adult ward. It is estimated that being treated on a Teenage Cancer Trust unit increases survival rates of patients by 15 percent, and this unit, I believed, would help create miracles and beat these cancers into a hasty retreat.

In the UK, six teenagers a day are diagnosed with cancer. The world of teenage cancer can be a dark one. Teens are isolated from friends, and cut off from the normal things kids do every day. They need a place that can help them feel as "normal" as possible while being treated. When you're a teenager, all you want is to fit in, right? This was one reason why the new unit was designed specially for thirteen-to-eighteen-year-olds and included a kitchen and dining area, a parents' room, a complementary therapy room, and access to the Internet and television. We wanted to let these kids have as normal a life as we could give them. To not treat them as teenagers with cancer, but as teenagers who are incredibly alive.

As a patron, my job was to raise funds and awareness to fight and treat teenage cancer. We raised three million dollars for the new unit, which replaced the original six-bed Teenage Cancer Trust ward that I opened in October 1997.

I would visit with every teenager before I left; I refused to be rushed off. Being a mother myself, somehow I could read into them, and we had loving one-on-one conversations. I sat very close to each teen, held their hands, and chatted. The important bit is not

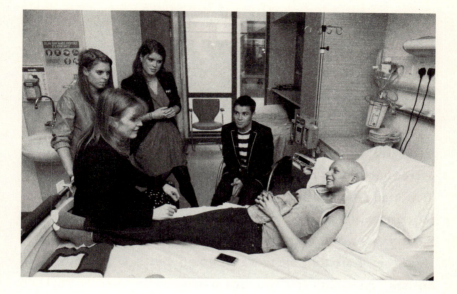

what I said—it is that these children needed to be heard. In some respects, listening is the single most important thing you can do. A small dose of such kindness can be powerful medicine. To see the delight on the faces of the teenagers makes you want to do all you can to help.

These were private, beautiful moments that no one could ever take away from me. Hearing their stories was inspirational and filled us all with a sense of hope.

After the opening of the unit, Beatrice and I took a train back to London. On my way home, my publicist, Kate Waddington, raised a red flag. Kate has been loyal and steadfast to me for more than twenty years. She had beautifully organized the unveiling of the Teenage Cancer Trust and coordinated all the media.

"Duchess, are you sure that Indian businessman was for real? I think you've been stung," she said.

It was only a phone call, but from a wonderful mood, I plunged into a bottomless abyss, suddenly feeling like I wanted to throw up. It just couldn't be true.

On Friday, Beatrice and I boarded a plane to attend Naomi Campbell's birthday party in the south of France. The party swung into action on Saturday night. At about 4:00 AM, Kate telephoned Beatrice. The chorus "Tonight's gonna be a good night" from the song "I Gotta Feeling" blared loudly as people happily danced, belying the crisis that was about to hit.

It was one of those phone calls you never forget.

"Mum, Kate told me it was a sting," Beatrice said. Her head drooped, like a flower too heavy for its stem.

The raggy tabloid *News of the World* had published an exposé of my meeting with the investor. All hell promptly broke loose. Beatrice and I hustled out of the party and took a 7:00 AM flight back to London.

The investor was none other than *News of the World* investigations editor Mazher Mahmood, who set up the sting and infiltrated my life by impersonating an executive. Also known as the "Fake Sheikh," Mahmood is a controversial figure who has targeted members of the Royal Family before.

As for the scoop about me, the tabloid's headline, in typical scummy fashion, blared: "Cash for Royal Access Sensation." Nearly the entire front page was plastered with a hazy photo of me, reaching out to seal the deal with a handshake. The news broke on Sunday, May 23, 2010.

The worldwide media swooped down on me like freshly killed prey. I was picked apart, pieces of my carrion strewn about like parking lot litter.

Beatrice became protective, asking over and over, "Why? Why were you set up this way?" Eugenie promised her complete support. In them I saw enormous courage and unconditional love, and it filled my heart until my shame broke it to bits.

A Buckingham Palace spokesman issued the following statement: "He [Prince Andrew] has carried out his role of Special Representative with complete and absolute propriety and integrity."

I apologized publicly for my "serious lapse of judgment" and added: "I can confirm that the Duke of York was not aware or involved in any of the discussions that occurred. I am sincerely sorry for my actions."

Deeply ashamed, but courageously determined to fulfill my commitments (my father insisted I always get back on a horse after a fall), I flew to Los Angeles for a charity dinner to accept the Catherine Variety Sheridan Award for my philanthropic work with underprivileged and disabled children. My darling daughter Beatrice had to pass the baton to Camilla, who had drawn the short straw to travel with me. Luckily, Camilla is steeped in kindness and her gracious, kind blue eyes willed me to hold on. During the flight to Los Angeles I sat bolt upright, an eye mask over my eyes, though really my eyes were wide open like those of a big gray horned owl. I was paralyzed by fear, unable to move. I was sure I would throw up even a cup of tea. I wanted to hide in the small lavatory and never come out. The flight attendant came up to me and asked me if I would like a drink. Looking into my eyes, she asked if I would like the whole bar! I had been crying so hard that my eyes were hazed over with sadness.

Once in LA I was a walking corpse, the Duchess in Disgrace, and I was acting out the part. How could I possibly face the people who had trusted me—and who were now honoring me? I felt like I had let so many people down.

Julia Morley and Cindy Charkow of the Variety Club, a group dedicated to improving the lives of children and young people everywhere, gave me the strength to get up onstage. I made a passing reference to the sting while accepting my award, saying, "I had a heavy day."

Nonetheless, the audience gave me a standing ovation. They didn't care about the scandal, or my trail of destruction. They believed in me, the person who cared about the plight of children the world over, and now they were expressing their gratitude. They had forgiven me when I felt I was unforgivable, when I could not forgive myself.

As I stepped off the stage, Simon Cowell whispered in my ear, "Come on, Fergie, you are a strong person. You can get through this. In fact, it makes you much more interesting!" Whether he meant those words or not, they raised my spirits.

Yet when the evidence of their reckless behavior is strewn like wreckage in the field of their lives, some people might have contemplated suicide. But that word is not in my vocabulary. I was in the gutter and when you get that low, the only place you can look is up. As Oscar Wilde so rightly says, the stars look good from the gutter. "We are all in the gutter, but some of us are looking at the stars."

After the scandal broke, Anne Keating, a stalwart friend and intrinsically good person whom I love, rang me with a suggestion.

"Get in touch with Ken Sunshine; he wants to help." Ken is a publicist in New York City. I called him.

"You must go on the *Oprah Winfrey Show* and explain your side of the story," Ken told me. I was both humbled and nervous, but definitely open to it. Ken next called his friend Jack Mori, who is one of Oprah's producers in Chicago.

On Tuesday, May 25, I was scheduled to launch my new series

of four children's books, the Helping Hand series, published by Sterling Publishing. I wrote the books to help children understand some of the personal and social issues they will have to deal with while growing up, including starting school, coping with bullying, learning about strangers, and losing loved ones. All children face new experiences as they grow up, and helping them understand and deal with each is one of the most demanding and rewarding things we do as parents. It was my hope that my books would encourage children and parents to talk about these issues.

As you can imagine, there was much discussion about whether I should participate in the launch, but I was determined not to let my publisher down. As my dad always said, "The show must go on." I was not about to let my disgrace from the *News of the World* sting get in my way of promoting these important books.

I pressed ahead with a busy schedule of public events, including BookExpo America, a lunch with the directors of Barnes & Noble, a cocktail reception with the book trade, and a book signing. Oscar Wilde also said, "Every saint has a past and every sinner has a future."

As I moved from event to event, I was constantly besieged by the paparazzi and press but I kept on going. Most demanding of all, I hosted a breakfast for 1,500 BookExpo delegates at which I had to introduce a number of other authors as well as speak about my Helping Hand books. Trying to be as calm and confident as I could be, I poked a little fun at myself. One of my Helping Hand books is entitled *Ashley Learns About Strangers*. "Perhaps I should have taken my own advice," I remarked ruefully.

Chris Ambler, my book publicist, and Marcus Leaver, president of Sterling, said something to me about my "strength of will" in going through with all this, while I had so many other personal and professional pressures to deal with. They kept telling me, "Just try and stay positive," and basically that's what I did. Their advice and support got me through the book tour.

Meanwhile, the call from Ken to Jack resulted in the miraculous: an invitation to appear on the *Oprah Winfrey Show* and explain myself before millions of viewers. At the time it seemed the right venue, and safe, because the show was to be taped on a closed set. Many of my friends thought I was making a huge mistake. They advised me to go away and not talk to anyone for six months, saying I was too raw and ill prepared to speak out publicly. Perhaps they were right, but I had no intention of doing so.

My head was hung so low when I got to Oprah's studios in Los Angeles that it was practically between my knees, as if I were struggling to regain my breath. I was dazed and in a fog. A lawyer friend of mine, Eric Cowan, called and told me that he would help me get through the interview. His wife, Mary, agreed: that on no account would he leave my side. This was true friendship.

I received much-needed support from other corners. Another dear friend, Linda Medvene, welcomed me with love and warmth. Linda is a well-known wardrobe specialist in LA. She would help me stand tall for my appearance on the *Oprah* show.

Despite being propped up by such dear friends, I found myself adrift in Oprah's questions throughout the one-hour interview, because I had so few answers. I had not yet begun to work on myself, evidenced by the fact that I had not even watched the video when I arrived on set.

Five minutes into the taping, Oprah insisted I watch it. Seeing my meeting with Mahmood through the eye of a camera made it real, not surreal. Asked how I felt, I said I pitied "her"—"her" being Sarah, the same troubled girl from long ago. I didn't even know who I was because I had lost myself.

As I watched the video, I felt so sad for that person, but that person was me. I was a mess.

When the show aired days later, the public response was unanimously and resoundingly negative. I'd hoped to set the record straight, and got a good kick instead. Everyone found my account vacuous and convoluted, and I suppose it was, except that every bit of what I said was true. My business and personal affairs were indeed vacuous and convoluted, because for years I'd been weaving elaborate webs trying to please people and avoid my deepest fears. Now rejection, failure, shame, and abandonment had all come home to roost.

My actions were the result of yet another visit from two demons, "Lapse in Judgment" and "Self-Sabotage," both terrifying figures who look like something that might haunt the Hogwarts corridors in the scarier Harry Potter books.

When Lapse in Judgment and Self-Sabotage choose to materialize, they strike hard at all my weaknesses, then fade away until next time. I am left with a level of regret and guilt that I cannot even begin to express in words, as well the distress of knowing I've let innumerable people down.

Only days before, I had been buoyant, happy, and hopeful about the future. Chances to blossom and bloom awaited me, of this I had been sure.

Another businessman, a legitimate one, had agreed to put up capital money to help my company grow and flourish. It was all very exciting and wonderful. He was so happy to meet Beatrice and see such a huge creative output of product and ideas that I have developed over many years. He was excited that many of these products and ideas could be successfully grown into a profitable business over the coming few years. I could not believe that he felt what is behind my passion for life and my ambition to succeed in creating a business, which can also assist in funding my charitable works.

He wanted to meet again very soon, in fact, in the next few days.

But it wasn't to be.

The day after the scandal broke, the businessman disappeared into the mist. He really wanted nothing more to do with me at all. In fact he said, "Sadly, it looks like you've hung yourself, and I will be unable to help you."

My reversal of fortune, my warp-speed descent into a hell of shame, was totally my own fault. I had made some big, stupid, careless, undisciplined, indelible mistakes before, but I suppose you can say this one was monstrously epic. Why hadn't I listened to my gut instinct? Why, why, why?

For the full flavor of my despair, let me share with you an entry from my diary during that time.

DIARY ENTRY

> *This morning, after a horrific dream of punishment, I started on a nightmare road of worthless and negative thoughts, namely the greedy ego wolf that is eating at my goodness, kindness, and tenderness. And forgiveness, too.*
>
> *I thought of so many "what ifs," that I drove myself into the bread bin, mayonnaise pot, sausages, and sausage rolls with ketchup. I yearned for soft-boiled eggs with "soldiers"—white toasted bread cut up into long fingers so you can dip the toast into the egg yolk—nursery food from*

when I was a little girl. I even reached out to seek reassurance from a suitor, who after reading such a needy email as mine, will go running into his cave.

I have struggled so hard that I resorted to sleep. I am unable to fathom or see further than my own nose at the moment, and this troubles me. I obviously have an excruciating fear of not knowing how to survive going forward. As I don't know how I will earn a living any longer, I need to rest, but I have to buy food, and I don't have any money. I must trust . . . I know. God will provide what I need. So today's lesson is total trust, and also to believe in myself. And to allow myself to heal.

I felt like I had jumped off a train bound for happiness, fulfillment, and success, then thrown a hand grenade at it and watched as the train went up in flames. Of all the epitaphs I've ever considered, *I shot myself in the foot again* says it all.

From: Simon

To: Sarah

Everybody makes mistakes. You just make yours rather more publicly than others. We do not judge and we accept you as you are as we always have done. Many receive advice, very few benefit. So I will not try to give you any. It was bad luck to be taken by that reporter. I'm glad it wasn't me . . . I would have suggested a million!

Hey ho . . . on we go!

Love,

Simon

From: Sarah

To: Simon

My dear Simon,

Thank you so much for your kindness. You have given me a lot to re-flect on, and I was so relieved to hear you are still my friend.

As of this moment, I am head down with embarrassment at my stupidity, my naïveté, and ignorance. I let myself down badly and be-trayed myself. I am not in self-pity or any of that. I just messed up, big.

I need to repair myself, and then the outside damage. Thankfully, when I do, you will be there again, to make me cry with laughter.

My prince and my girls are right behind me, and thank heavens for that.

With lots of love,

Fergie

2 | *Journey*

The world is not such a bad place, as long as you don't take it too seriously.

$\mathcal{O}$VER THE YEARS, I have been through several serious personal crises. I always managed to survive them, in part because I could always engross myself in my work and my family, and not think about pain I did not want to feel. I am at a stage in my life, however, where this just does not work anymore. I want to go deeper and further and come to terms with my life and with myself in ways that I had always studiously avoided.

And so, I have to embark on a journey to find myself. Some of my critics might think that's not much of a find. But to find myself is to find life itself, to recognize parts of me that are valuable and precious, because, deep down, I believe myself worth finding—and saving.

Along the way, I must answer important questions . . . Am I really who I say I am? Why do I keep making the same mistakes over and over? How can I change the self-destructive patterns of the past? Can I look deeply inside and think about the implications for my life?

I know this is going to be one of those bumpy, surprising trips in which detours are a frequent part of the journey. But as we hit bumps in the road, reality sets in and we learn that no matter how hard we try, there are some things we aren't prepared for. A blind alley here, a detour there—they are all part of the journey. All we can control is the way we choose to react in each situation. Mine will be a journey about naming and befriending the detours, road signs, storms, obstacles and shelters along the way, and it will be a journey where the old maps no longer apply.

I will go forward with whatever self-compassion I can muster. By nature, I am very hard on myself. When I am self-critical, I treat myself in ways I would never want to treat someone I love. I beat myself up for every imperfection, I punish myself for any weakness, and I discourage myself from going after what I really want.

Intuitively, I know that whether you want to change a negative behavior (like overeating) or commit to a positive one (like meditating every day), the best approach is to cultivate self-compassion and tap into its power, so that you can stick to your resolutions—and build a better life.

I understand, fully and honestly, that becoming whole is a process, not a lesson learned in hours or days. I will always be a work in progress. Self-transformation does not happen overnight.

I believe, too, that our future is defined by our past. Like everyone else in the world, I've gone through periods of great sadness. I never looked deeply enough at the pain from my past. I never tried to understand that pain and work through it, and now I was paying the price of an unexamined life. It was all a journey I had avoided, but one I now must take. And so, my voyage of self-discovery must start here with a little detour into my past.

Most of you know me as Fergie or perhaps the Duchess of York. Google my name—and yes, I confess I've done that—and more often than not I am linked to some tabloid scandal or crisis. But what about all the other things I've been?

I've been a spokesperson, writer, film producer, photographer, artist, pilot, and entrepreneur. I am a mother. I'm also a charity patron, humanitarian, and children's rights advocate. I've even worked as a waitress and a ski instructor. So much of this seems dwarfed by the various predicaments I've found myself in and the distortions of my sensationalized life.

I was born to a mother, the former Susan Wright, who was typical of upper-class British women—brought up to marry well and be society wives. Few highborn women raised their own children; typically, child-rearing was left to nannies, tutors, governesses, and boarding schools.

My mother was raised at Powerscourt, the Wingfield family's ancestral home in Ireland—a commanding one hundred–room mansion perched atop a mile-long driveway ringed by hills and forests and crowned by one of Europe's most renowned gardens. A series of terraces leads the eye onward to the distinctive slopes of the Sugar Loaf Mountain.

Now open to the public, Powerscourt is one of the most beautiful country estates in Ireland—the Versailles of Ireland, really. Drive through arched iron gates and down a beech-lined drive, and you'll pass parklands, gardens, lakes, and fountains on your way to the estate.

Powerscourt's opulence belied the fact that my mother's childhood wasn't entirely pampered. Her parents were strict, demanding, and unsentimental. As a baby, Mum was cared for by a nanny and was then passed to a governess whose job was to instill refinement and discipline. At age twelve my mother entered a proper boarding school for girls and then an elite finishing school. She was known as a brilliant equestrian at fifteen, debuted before the Queen at seventeen, and by her nineteenth birthday she was married to my father, Ronald Ferguson, who was a suitable match socially and with whom she shared a passion for horses and polo.

By the time I was born in 1959, the Wright family's glory days were drawing to a close. I was barely four when my grandmother sold Powerscourt, making my older sister, Jane, and me the first generation of girls on my mother's side to grow up "outside the gates," so to speak.

Mother was an extraordinary person, exuberant and generous, famous for her beauty and charm that instantly lit up a room. Jane and I agree that our mother instilled in us a sense of noblesse oblige that neither of has forgotten and which, to some extent, still shapes our lives. Mum used to say to us: "Now, when you're walking down the street, and you're looking for sweets in a shop, or toys in a shop, always look around and see if you can help someone cross the road, or something like that!"

Mum was at her best teaching us the things she loved, like raising and riding horses, skiing, and hosting parties. Yet she seemed befuddled by the mundane responsibilities of homemaking and child-rearing. My mother could not stand baby talk, and she had even less patience for crying or pouting—and no tolerance at all for bouts of weakness or fears of failure. Mum had a narrow view of her role as a mother: her duty was to turn out well-groomed, well-rounded, beautifully mannered children. Perfect was the standard Mum was raised to, and that made it the standard for my sister Jane and me.

I felt most happy and secure when I was at school. Since kindergarten I'd attended nearby Daneshill school, as gentle and nurturing a place as I've ever known. I was liked by my teachers and had lots of friends.

I was nine when my family moved to Dummer Down, the dairy farm my father inherited in 1969 when my grandfather passed away of leukemia. It is located over the county line in Hampshire, in the village of Dummer, about an hour's drive from London.

Apart from having a funny name, the village of Dummer is a quaint, tiny clutch of thatched-roof cottages, with a small stone church, a post office, a pub, and a country store. The name of the village, by the way, is derived from Dun (meaning hill) and Mer (lake or pond). A winding lane, canopied with cherry trees and just right for bicyclists and toboggans, leads to Dummer Down, a redbrick Queen Anne house with beamed ceilings, a large country oven, and several bedrooms. The house sits regally over glorious views of the loveliest parts of rural England.

I was always one to be outdoors, chafing for adventure in all weather, and Dummer Down gave me a kingdom to explore: more than eight hundred acres of gently swelling pasture and woodland. We had black-and-white Frisian milk cows and a neat field of corn, barley, oats, and wheat. There was a rose garden and an apple orchard, which doubled as a dog cemetery. Flowers grew everywhere: pink fuchsia, lavender foxgloves, blankets of white and yellow daffodils. We had everything we could possibly want.

For Jane and me, the exciting part of rural life was our expanded pony operation. Dummer Down had brick and cedar stables and a two-sided barn, open in the middle—a sort of animal courtyard. We had an equitation "school"—a fenced-off grassy circle for training the horses, and, best of all, a full-fledged cross-country course, complete with tiger traps—three wooden poles placed over a fence—for jumping.

When I was ten years old, my mother suffered a late-term miscarriage and nearly died. Our family was on holiday at a ski resort. At about 7 PM, my friend Camilla and I wandered away from everyone and went into a store to look around. Mum was so worried that she had lost us. There was great relief when she found us, though in her haste she slipped on the ice and fell.

It wasn't until we came back to England and Dad rushed her to the hospital that my mother was treated for toxemia, a life-threatening condition that affects pregnant women.

After she was released from the hospital, we felt that Mum blamed us for her loss. Jane and I did not even know she was pregnant. The revelation was a shock to my little ten-year-old mind. I was tormented by guilt.

My parents later told us the baby was in heaven and offered no further details. In the months that followed, my mother was pale and expressionless, spending days secluded in her bedroom. Meanwhile, my father went about business as usual, managing the Duke of Edinburgh's polo club. When Dad would pop in and out of our house between matches, he was reliably cheery and attentive. Mum did not share his cheer and did her best to ignore him.

In the summer of 1972, my parents flew out on holiday to the Ionian island of Corfu. They invited their friend Hector Barrantes, an Argentinean polo player, who had lost his wife in a car crash. Mum fell deeply in love with him, and the ensuing quake would rattle Dummer Down and all of our lives.

I remember the time Mum organized one last Christmas, complete with paper hats and crackers and much contrived jollity. Soon thereafter, she began shuttling to London, where my family had a small house in Chelsea, and going on trips with Hector. By the following autumn, she would move out of Dummer for good.

In the meantime, I had my own transition—and trauma—to deal with: changing schools. I'd been sheltered at Daneshill with close friends I still claim today. Sadly, Daneshill was a primary school that did not go beyond the sixth grade.

When the time came to pick a senior school for me in the fall of 1972, my parents settled on nearby Hurst Lodge School in Sunningdale, where Jane was already enrolled. I was to be a weekly boarder, with weekends back at Dummer—and I was devastated. My friends had moved on to St. Mary's School in Wantage, Oxfordshire.

Hurst Lodge was known as Britain's premier school for aspiring ballerinas, making it a peculiar choice for me. I'd aspired to be an Olympic show jumper, not a dancer. Forget that I bore no resemblance to the other Hurst Lodge girls, who were lithe and diminutive. I was nearly five foot seven inches tall, with a curly ginger mop and freckles galore. With my tutu, black leotard, and hair in a tight bun, I wore rugby socks—not exactly the sort of costume for a ballerina! But the pink tights I had to wear made me itch, and the socks helped relieve the itching. Also, I thought they were quite practical, as I would play basketball after dance class. This fashion faux pas was to be the demise of my ballet career. The day I decided to wear the dreaded rugby socks was the day we were to greet one of Europe's prima ballerinas. This so outraged the school's founder, Doris Stainer, that she whisked me out of the studio and banned me from ballet. I would truly miss my ballet class, but when Doris Stainer banished me, there would be no appeal for forgiveness.

Nonetheless I was very successful at school. I was made "head girl"—which is the equivalent of class president. I was winning netball captain. I was our class ringleader, too, gregarious and dramatic with a flair for stirring up mischief. One parents' weekend I had my friends drape loo roll all over the schoolyard telephone poles and wires that came from them while I spiked the lavatory faucets and drinking fountains with vegetable dye. The Hurst Lodge staff was incandescent with rage about the stunt and knew all too well who had masterminded it. I expected I'd be suspended or worse when I was summoned to the dean's office. What I got was the usual schoolmarm's scolding and a disciplinary notice mailed to my father.

By my antics you'd think I enjoyed being a renegade when in truth I was crying out for help because of my disintegrating family life. I desperately wanted someone, anyone, to ask me why I acted the way I did. I'd gratefully have unloaded the turmoil clouding my head: I hated the way I looked, I felt silly and awkward around boys, and I was worried about things at home. Florence, my best friend at school, said I cried every night.

Mum moved to London to start a new life, and soon this included Hector. Everybody adored Hector, and as I got to know him so did I. He was a big man physically and bigger than life in all the ways that made Mum sparkle again.

Late in 1973, Mum returned from a stay in Argentina with Hector to see if she could live there for good. She came out to Dummer one weekend. Jane and I could see the purpose in her stride, the way her legs moved in her brown velvet trousers. She walked straight past us to see Dad in his drawing room and shut the door behind her. My sister and I stood mute and rooted in the hallway, waiting on a decision we had no say in.

We heard harsh words behind the closed door of my father's drawing room. It was an astonishing moment for us, because my parents never fought out loud, but now insults and accusations were echoing throughout the house. Then silence until Mum came marching though the living room, headed for the front door.

Gripping a suitcase in each hand, she directed her parting salvo at Jane and me. Earlier in the day we had walked to the village hairdresser and had our ponytails lopped off. My hair was closely cropped in tightly wound red curls.

When Mum saw what we had done, she raised her voice at us, "I told you to never cut your hair!" She yanked the door open and then slammed it with such force that it took a huge painting down with a thunderous crash. I recall standing frozen in the foyer, shards of glass under my stocking feet, fixating on the spot where the picture had always hung. Mum had never, ever looked or sounded so angry before. I had no idea that she was divorcing my father, and that she was never going to walk through that front door again. I thought she was mad because Jane and I had cut our hair!

One moment I had a mother, and the next moment I had nothing. Absolutely nothing. I was convinced I was worthless, unlovable, and a fraud.

Her decision—"I've fallen in love, I'm leaving my daughters and moving to another country"—left an awful feeling in my young mind. I wondered: "Am I not good enough? Am I not lovable enough? Was I somehow to blame?" I believe that when she abandoned us, I lost my self-worth.

The day Mum left for the airport, I pretended I was overjoyed. She deserved to be happy, I thought, and I was not going to ruin it for her. Inside I felt a devastating loss—so devastating, in fact, that I felt like I was tied up in barbed wire and walking on hot coals. Worse, I put myself in an institution of my own making, shutting away and abandoning the little Sarah I had been. "She" caused my mother to leave, so she must be bad, so let's lock her away like a lunatic and never let her out. That is how I lived the rest of my life.

Right after my mother left, I rode my pony to a candy shop. Completely unprepared for the crushing sense of grief and loss, I began, blindly, furiously, to binge on sweets—a desperate, unconscious attempt to mute the crazy-making pain. Then Dad sold the pony, and I was even more heartbroken.

By my fourteenth birthday, Jane was mostly steering clear of the glum scene at Dummer Down. After leaving school for secretarial college, she minded a shop for a time. Later, when I was sixteen, Jane would further flee to marry a fellow named Alex Makim and live on his sheep ranch in Australia.

With Mum out of our lives, Dad traveling all the time, and my sister suddenly married and living in Australia, our home, Dummer Down House, stood like a time capsule, perfectly decorated just as my mother had left it. Dad hired a new housekeeper and instructed her to keep the cupboards stocked with my favorite treats. With no one home and nothing to do, I'd dip in and out of the kitchen all day long. For me, eating seemed to chase away the blues, at least for a little while.

Poor Dad had to take on the burdens of being a single parent—both with little experience for the work and no firsthand example or memory to draw upon. He was really in way over his head. But Dad and I were in this together. I could not let him down—I knew he was suffering in spirit—so I took on the full responsibility of running the household for him. It amazes me sometimes that we came through it.

I tried my best at school, but cried every night. I led a gray life. Even my riding fell off. I didn't do it as properly as I used to. Mum's leaving stole much of the fun from it. I missed her so much. I had been just thirteen when she'd left. Entering puberty, I had no feminine influence in my life. No one showed me how to dress or wear makeup. No one explained what makes a marriage or doesn't. No one told me what it was to be a woman. I was left confused, sad, and abandoned.

Nevertheless, Dad gave our home discipline and stability, and I liked the fact that someone big, strong, and smart was there for me.

Mum and Dad divorced in 1974. Mum and Hector were married a year later and that was that.

Dad held on. He never gave in, never succumbed to languor or self-pity, never failed to go off to work. He sustained a formidable social life, going to dinners and other events. My father loved women, too, and I wanted him to marry again. Eventually, he met his second wife, also called Susan (Deptford). She was much younger than Dad and much closer to Jane and me in age. Susan is a kind, loving woman who has been one of the most important people in my life. We love her dearly.

When they met, she was a Norfolk farmer's daughter, cooking directors' lunches in London; he a former Life Guards officer working as Prince Charles's polo manager. Tall and blond, with classic English gentlewoman's good looks, the young Susan bore a strong resemblance to the movie star Grace Kelly when she first met my father. They were married in November 1976, and had three children, Andrew, Alice, and Eliza.

After I graduated from Hurst Lodge, I set out, at seventeen years old, on an adventure to crisscross America by Greyhound bus. I had my father's blessing, but not his financial backing, so I had to work my way from city to city. One of my most memorable stops was Squaw Valley, a ski resort in California. It is a place where cliffs loom over the toy village at the bottom, and above the rock outcroppings a broad lap of meadows basks in permanent sunshine. Lifts were everywhere, and little chalets, built out of cedar and redwood, dotted the hillside.

I worked as a waitress at the local strudel shop and as a human ski lift for children who were disabled. I stayed with Jessie Huberty, a very dear friend of my mother's, and her son Martin, truly a gem of a person. I was still hurting over Mum's abandonment. Jessie wrapped her arms around me and gave me strength and hope. She liked to say, "Cream always rises to the top, and, honey, you are the cream of the crop! Don't you forget it!"

Martin is an accomplished film producer and a steadfast friend. He travels with me part of the year to help me with my projects. He works closely with me to make sure all the pieces come together and that we're going to be in the right place at the right time.

After the road trip to America and a successful stint at secretarial college, I entered the working world with good skills and courage to take on life. What I lacked in confidence I more than made up for with my well-honed talent for people-pleasing, which helped me land my first job—in public relations, naturally. However, I had let myself get so caught up in how other people saw me that I had little sense of how I saw myself. In a very real way, I had lost sight not only of myself but of what mattered to me.

For sure I was a hapless bachelorette unable to cook a meal, coordinate an outfit, or manage my finances. As someone who detested being home alone, I threw myself into London's club scene; life in the fast lane suited me because the quicker I moved, the less I had to think about myself and my future. I just lived for every moment with energy and love.

In the spring of 1985, I found a heavy bond envelope in my postal slot. It was from the Royal Household, requesting "the pleasure of your company at the Queen's house party at Windsor Castle during the week of Royal Ascot."

As I would learn later, the mysterious invitation turned out to be the matchmaking work of my distant cousin and childhood friend Diana Spencer, by then HRH Princess Diana, who believed Prince Andrew, the Queen's second son, and I would get along famously.

I arrived at Windsor on June 18. A footman met me at the castle's private entrance to take my luggage. A lady-in-waiting led me through corridors of rooms to my room, a major bit of exercise. There, a lovely, friendly girl, a housemaid named Louise, would take care of me the whole length of my stay. I doubt I would have made it without her.

On my bedside table was a card embossed with the Queen's cipher, listing the four-day schedule of mealtimes for the day. For lunch I had been placed between a vice admiral and Prince Andrew, then on leave from his duties on the HMS *Brazen.* I knew Andrew from my childhood days, when we'd played tag together, and since then I had seen him occasionally.

I stepped into the Green Drawing Room at 12:45 on the dot for drinks. At 1 PM I took my place at a table long enough for shuffle-board: thirteen people on each side, one on each end. For the duration of the meal, conversation followed basic protocol; following the Queen's lead, the ladies would speak to the man on their right or their left, alternating with each course.

When I turned to face Andrew, I was struck by how handsome he was. He was easy to talk to and I felt very relaxed with him, even though I addressed him as "Sir," as per protocol.

Out of such humble beginnings, a whirlwind romance soon ensued and a year later we were engaged.

In Andrew I found my perfect man and soul mate. He was relaxed and endlessly charming, a prankster like me, yet solid and kind. In me, I suppose Andrew saw a wildflower—a bubbly and forthright woman without pretense or motives. Together we were like well-matched bookends, pleasant to look at and equally supportive of one another.

As man and wife, we were the Duke and Duchess of York, and together we seemed an unbeatable team. Andrew was a dashing naval officer working on active duty. I aspired to be a relatable princess—fresh and friendly, compassionate with a common touch.

Mind you, I still had no self-confidence, but I was genuine in my desire to represent a new kind of Royal. Having spent half my life being a tireless people-pleaser I felt ready to assume my public role. The world stage proved no place for someone like me with deep insecurities and a penchant for self-sabotage. Even before our wedding, I found royal life monumentally challenging. There are no books on how to be a proper princess. I'd counted on having

Andrew at my side to teach me the ropes, but to our amazement, following our honeymoon the palace courtiers had Andrew sent off to sea, and relinquished me to being incarcerated in a dimly lit suite on the second floor of Buckingham Palace. Most people think that would be fine, but what they don't understand is that the palace is a Department of Environment building. So, for example, on September 1, the radiators get turned on. It is a government building, not a home, and you must keep to its rules and regulations. If you don't put in your order for meals and the kitchen is closed for the night, then that's it.

All of this left me to navigate the cadre of palace courtiers whose job it was to run my life and keep me up to standards, a formidable challenge for someone accustomed to winging it. During the first five years of our marriage, I saw my beloved Andrew only forty days a year.

In 1988, I learned that I was pregnant. In August, Andrew came home on two weeks' leave and our baby was induced on August 8 to fit the Royal Navy's schedule. Beatrice went into a stressed situation halfway down the birth canal and my obstetrician said we were sixty seconds away from a cesarean section. Thankfully she continued on happily to a normal birth, though I had an epidural. I'm eternally grateful that Andrew was there throughout, holding my hand. I couldn't have wished to have someone more special or more calm by side.

As a new mother, I was a complete novice, never having so much as bathed a younger sibling or worked a day as a mother's helper. But when I looked into my daughter's sweet face and huge eyes, I felt such overwhelming pride. Her complete dependence on me infused my life with a divine energy hitherto unknown. We named her Beatrice after Queen Victoria's youngest daughter.

In September, when Beatrice was six weeks old, I left her with Alison Wardley to join Andrew on tour in Australia. I had urgently wanted to take her with me; newborns are highly portable, after all. You strap them to your chest, and off you both go.

But in the eyes of the palace establishment, it was ill advised to take Beatrice to Australia. Despite my misgivings, I knew Beatrice would be well cared for by Alison, and so I left. That's when the press turned on me, branding me a bad mother.

Never mind that I was tired and out of shape—corpulent from the weight I'd gained in my first pregnancy. The press made a mockery out of that, too. When the press ridicules you, it's grueling, sad, and dreadful on your heart, and you feel an acute sense of loneliness.

Perhaps I was trying to prove something by the time Eugenie came along. I was in great shape then from swimming every day and working with a marvelous trainer named Josh Saltzman, who put me through my paces by making me go up and down the palace stairs. Well, it worked. I could get into my size 12 jeans, and I wore a size 12 suit to the hospital on the day Eugenie was born. Josh saved my life many a time with his friendship and encouragement. In the darkest hours, when I wanted to give up on myself, Josh would say, "Get back on the bike!"

After Eugenie was born, I spent more time at home with both my daughters, only to have the media accuse me of being work-shy. I could not win. Five years after my marriage, I went from being a Royal darling feted by the media as a "breath of fresh air" to the most criticized female member of the Royal Family.

Andrew and I carried on in our two distinct worlds. By 1989 we were sharing less and less until we lost the stitch of the fabric we'd been weaving together. A marriage is not about special events or lavish holidays; it's about small things, all those mundane moments that add up to something more.

Under the saddest of circumstances, after ten years of marriage, Andrew and I decided we could not go on as husband and wife. Our marriage did not fail because we stopped loving each other. It failed largely because the absences gradually destroyed us. We rarely saw each other, and you cannot build a foundation without the bricks and mortar of togetherness and communication.

To this day, Andrew and I both believe that we would still be married had we fought for what we believed was right. When people asked if I could cope with naval life, I replied: "Of course! You can cope with anything if you love your man."

I would have followed him anywhere. But I was disillusioned after being refused permission to live with Andrew in married quarters where he was stationed.

We both discussed the possibility of Andrew's leaving the navy and becoming governor of Canada for a bit. Looking back, if Andrew and I had been strong enough to say that we were going to do something like that, we probably would still be together now.

In hindsight, I regret we did not make a stronger case for Andrew to leave the navy. My people-pleasing and approval-seeking behavior kicked in, and I did not think he would be happy to leave the navy for me. I did not fight hard for that, as I did not want him to think badly of me.

We were young, immature in many ways. He didn't want to rock the boat. It is very difficult to stand up for things if you're still growing up.

I love him as much today as I did then, as does he love me. The saddest part of the story is that it needn't have ended as it did.

The days following our separation were truly dark; leaving the royal fold as I did makes you a non-person and a pariah. I love Britain, and I loved being a princess. I was very good at it, dedicated to giving my life to duty and to my country.

But I felt discarded, as if I no longer belonged. As much as I cared about what people thought of me, I had to shut that from my mind and concentrate on what really mattered. Beatrice and Eugenie were born to royalty and for that they needed a very good mummy. I was willing to do anything to be that.

From there on, I threw myself into my charity work for sick, neglected, and abused children—all children around the world, really. That is what my life is all about. It is a passion inspired by my grandmother—whom I affectionately called "Grummy." Although she was from an old and prosperous family, and herself very much a stern parent to my mother, the fact is that my grandmother had a heart of gold and enormous compassion for those who were less fortunate.

She was a big fan of St. Francis of Assisi. Whenever I would slip into one of my woebegone moods, Grummy would tap me lovingly on the forehead and quote the Prayer of St. Francis:

Lord, make me an instrument of your peace.
Where there is hatred, let me sow love.
Where there is injury, pardon.
Where there is doubt, faith.
Where there is despair, hope.
Where there is darkness, light.
Where there is sadness, joy.
O Divine Master,

grant that I may not so much seek to be consoled, as to
  console;
to be understood, as to understand;
to be loved, as to love.
For it is in giving that we receive.
It is in pardoning that we are pardoned,
and it is in dying that we are born to Eternal Life.
Amen.

Seeing my misery, she would add that "when you feel bad about yourself, give to others," and her advice made me see the self-indulgence of my brooding.

Writing down the good things I've done rescues me from self-doubt, and so one day while feeling very melancholy, I penned these words in my diary:

In 1992, I took myself off to the most polluted place in Po-land, Upper Silesia, and found that the only hospital for children was in a place where all the coal factories were— Katowice. The children there were dying from cancer from breathing polluted air. How could they get better with no clean air?

I met a charismatic, bright, and superbly talented and strong Irish girl named Sophie Lillingston. She was so enthu-siastic, and she had been working tirelessly with the amazing doctors and nurses of the Children's Hospital in Katowice. I immediately grasped an ounce of her enthusiasm and wanted to start Children in Crisis, a charity for forgotten children, straight away in order to help Sophie realize her dream.

The doctors and nurses in Poland in 1992 had very lim-

ited medical supplies and support, through no fault of their own. There were very little available resources back then.

Visiting time for the children was just one hour—not enough time for the parents working in the factories to visit them. It was on that trip that I founded Children in Crisis.

We were able to move the children to the Tatra Mountains where the air was pure. Experts say that 28 days of clean air bestows 2 more years of life. Children in Crisis built a wonderful facility there called Mountain Haven.

To this day, 32 children a month travel to Mountain Haven to breathe, to laugh, to cook marshmallows on an open fire. I would give my last pennies and my last hours to keep that facility going. In fact, the week prior to the Fake Sheikh scandal, I was in Poland to raise money to keep the facility open.

Today we have approximately 43 schools in places like Sierra Leone and Afghanistan. Had that horrible Fake Sheikh told the truth, you would have heard the videotape saying that I needed £110,000 to build a girls' school in Afghanistan.

After the Oklahoma City bombing, we pledged $150,000 for the pediatric center there. I became personally involved, meeting P. J. Allen, the little boy who was so badly burned he wasn't able to go outside for two years. We gave his family fifteen thousand dollars to build a little greenhouse so he could run around and play. I love P. J. I saw him recently when I went back to Oklahoma City.

In total humility, I say that one day, after I'm gone, people will know that I dedicated my life to children's causes. My family knows this now, as do the children in the countries where I have built schools. They know.

———

So much of who I am can be attributed to all these roots—my family, my friends, my upbringing, my charities. I carry my roots deep within me. I had always believed they were my strength when things got tough. Yet, looking back, where were they in May 2010?

> From: Simon
> To: Sarah
> Darling Ferg,
> From you for a while, except to your sworn closest mates and family, what the world needs is "silence." People do forget and, strangely, they also forgive, but not if you won't let them.
> Into the shadows you must go and re-emerge on a sunny day, quietly doing something really lovely, like attending one your daughters' weddings . . . not with a triumphant march as a Roman general returning victoriously to Rome. No front-stage stuff.
> Understand that affection is won through quiet humility . . . really understand this. There is nothing greater in a human and nothing rarer, and nothing worth more.
> Reputation takes a long time to get back and it is the most valuable thing to have in life. So you have time and make it your goal. It is really the only thing of value you can pass on to your children and grandchildren. So get it back, slowly.
> Remember the words of the Bard:
>
> "The purest treasure mortal times afford, is spotless reputation; that away, men are but gilded loam or painted clay."
>
> Much love,
> Simon

To: Simon

From: Sarah

My dearest Simon,

As coal under pressure turns into a diamond, our spirit under great pressure has the chance to turn into the jewel that it is. This has always been known.

The weight of things brings us to our knees, and we are forced to see the underside, and there the light of God shines. I am looking at my whole life. I am trying to see my thousands of flaws from the underside, and to go forward from there.

I am resolving what needs to be resolved, and I will return to full energy and the really good old Ferg from all those years ago.

As to anything else, I am battling hard through each day, but your words made me weep with joy. I felt relieved by your strength and humor. But more than anything, I felt your great compassion and kindness for your old mate.

All love,

The bloody Fool

Fergs

From: Peter

To: Sarah

June 23, 2010

Dear Sarah,

Just a short note from your Mountain Haven friends to tell you how enormously grateful we are for all that you have done (and selflessly given) for Polish children over so many years. You have been a rock and an inspiration for us all and we hope that in this difficult time for you, you will know that you are in our thoughts and hearts, and al-

ways welcome in our homes, whether in London, Zakopane, or Lipnica Wielka. All you need to do is call, or drop in—anytime.

With much love and best wishes,
Peter

From: Simon
To: Sarah
What matters is NOW. The present is the only time we live in. It's REAL time. The past has been. The future does not need to overconcern us because a drunken bus driver can end it at ten o'clock tomorrow morning. It is NOW. The present, which is a word meaning "gift." Never forget this, and make the best of it in every way, every day.

I must not lecture and do not mean to. I am your friend. I am over seventy and am allowed to speak my mind!

Love,
Simon

To: Simon
From: Sarah
My dearest Simon,
I totally get what you are saying, and I am working flat out on the inner Sarah and returning with total humility.

I love you now and always for your total objective candor and extraordinary strength of friendship. Your words make me think a lot. One day you will be proud of me.
Thank you so much.

All my love,
Ferg

3 | *The Lotus Flower*

I went to find the lotus flower within myself.

I WANTED MY ROOTS to be like those of the lotus flower. It blossoms on the surface of still water, while its roots go right down to the mud below. Untouched by the dirty water in which it lives, the lotus remains strong, pure, and undefiled.

The lotus is one of my favorite plants—a most unusual plant—and I see it as a metaphor for the new life I hope to build on this journey.

The first time I saw a lotus, it swayed precariously in the breeze. I imagined that an underwater juggler must be holding the bottom of several stems and balancing the leaves above water.

The lotus flower is a legendary symbol of life and endurance. Buddha is often depicted meditating in the lotus position, cradled by a lotus flower. Ulysses's crew mingled with lotus-eaters and, like them, became dreamy. Egyptian goddesses were symbolized by the lotus. Some Hindu sects see the world as a lotus flower, with the seven petals representing the seven divisions of heaven. The lotus was also the flower of Lilith, Adam's first wife in Jewish mythology.

In the middle of a lotus flower is a large cone-shaped seedpod; when dried and drooped it resembles a showerhead. The Chinese eat the seeds, believing them to be rejuvenating and aphrodisiacal.

If ever I felt less like a lotus flower, it was in the aftermath of the scandal. I was in muddy water, and I feared there was no way back from such grimy depths of disgrace. I could not trust anyone at all, except for my girls and Andrew, who stuck to me like glue. We are one unit, we are family, and there's no question about it. After the Fake Sheikh scandal, Andrew was my champion, my total champion. He is steadfast and loyal and true. He has always seen the real Sarah—which is why he still loves me as much as he does. And the girls are extraordinary. They know me, so they also know that the person who became emotionally, mentally, and physically bankrupt was not the person they knew as their mother.

Even so, I felt like I had to change, but I had no idea what to do. I needed to zero in on areas of my life that were falling apart and try to understand why. I knew that I would be stronger for it.

Self-knowledge requires depth, commitment to change, and endurance of what life can put us through. The lotus can offer us a lesson. Instead of beating ourselves up for what we did or didn't do, we need to see ourselves like the lotus, ascending above the grime toward the sunshine, blooming amid murky water, and emerging unscathed and unblemished from the muddy pond of the world. The sooner we touch base with the immortal lotus within, the more beneficent and mindful we shall be of our actions.

As it has many poets and artists, the flower's beauty inspired me to write the following poem to my daughters.

> *I dream that my daughters rise like the Lotus flower. That they grow to have strong and secure roots, to stand tall and steadfast. So that when the rain comes, storms hit, and the dusty winds blow—nothing sticks to their core.*

> *I dream that they face the fears of life, with the calm knowledge of the Divine Light of their own Guide within themselves. To be aware of the Golden energy of their own soul. I dream they take time to realize and know the truth is not outside but inside.*

> *I dream that they don't live with regrets, that they cannot let either the past or the future rob them, like thieves . . . of the present day.*

> *I dream that my daughters have courage to be exactly who they are, strong and bold, never to wear a blanket in order to hide the true golden beauty of themselves.*

*Your playing small does not serve the world. There is
   nothing enlightened about shrinking so that other people
   won't feel insecure around you.*

*We were born to make and manifest the glory of God
   within us. It is not just in some; it is in everyone.*

*And, as we let our own light shine, we consciously give other
   people permission to do the same.
As we are liberated from our fear, our presence
   automatically liberates others.*

*I dream that my daughters keep the lotus flower within
   them always.*

I dream my daughters walk with strength as they inspire
and lead by example of Goodness, Kindness, Humor,
Respect, Dignity, and solid Integrity to themselves.

If they lead with pride and humility, with good intentions,
the mirror energy of life will be reflected.

Like the lotus, precious things grow out of places that are not so precious. And so, I set about getting to the bottom of myself, resolving what needed to be resolved. I waded out and jammed my fragile roots into the muddy pond of the world.

From: Marcus

To: Sarah

The people who are the most messed up are the ones who don't admit it.

Spiritual truth: We all have issues, otherwise we wouldn't be in these bodies. We'd be flying around in other dimensions where the angels and the righteous live.

Today, when you're wishing you were like some perfect person you see on TV or in your graduation yearbook or in the mansion on the good side of the tracks, don't.

No one is better than you. No one is worse. No one.

Marcus

From: Charlie

To: Sarah

My darling Sarah,

Winston Churchill, after the war, was a special guest at a dinner at

Oxford. He got to make a speech. For the interminable time of two minutes, he said nothing. Then: "You should never give up! Never! Never! Never! Never!" After this, he sat down. The best speech I have ever heard.

You have been used for certain reasons by certain people. You were working for your cause. You did nothing wrong. I am appalled to see how far the new so-called journalism can go. You are a straight, wonderful human being. In the future, you should be more careful and think everyone could be an enemy. Except me, of course.

With much love,
Charlie

4 | *Far from the Madding Crowd*

You can take everything away from someone,
but you can't take away their spirit.

AFTER THE SCANDAL, I sought much-needed privacy, but not in the UK. People think London is my home, but in truth I live nowhere, and I live everywhere. In this book you will find me in many places, which is how I live my life. I do not have a home; it is as if I belong to no place. I like to be a nomad, traveling for business or charity work, and go where I feel like going.

But when I do touch down, it is at Royal Lodge, Windsor Great Park, a home bequeathed to Andrew by his grandmother, the late Queen Mother. The Lodge dates originally from the midseventeenth century and is today a thirty-room estate and Andrew's principal residence. For a time, though, I hid in the darkness of my Royal Lodge bedroom, comforted by the presence of my two daughters.

But I just could not sort my life out in London. I needed a change of place. I telephoned a close friend, Ana Marie Tavares, and asked her if she knew of anywhere I could go to heal, and sit away from "the madding crowd." Ana tried to get me into a brand-new spa in Phuket, Thailand, but the resort officials put their collective feet down: "We do not want a person like her to come here."

As you might imagine, it was a hurtful, crushing rejection. Worse yet, I agreed with, and internalized, the rejection, and I felt cursed.

Ana Marie would not, and did not, give up on me, or on her search for a suitable place where I could rest. She located a place in Portugal, Aquapura, and my stoically steadfast and kind assistant Amanda and I set off. You may think of such places as hangouts for the frivolous and indulgent, but many spas are more accurately described as healing retreats: They've become modern centers for physical, emotional, and spiritual growth—havens for people who need to regroup, rethink their approach to the world, and rededicate themselves to a healthy lifestyle. And that was exactly what I needed.

After we arrived, our driver maneuvered our vehicle along a narrow, twisting road toward the hilltop village of Provesende, in Portugal's Douro Valley. It is a seventy-mile swath of steep stone-terraced vineyards, where port wine has been made for centuries, and is some of the most beautiful countryside in the world.

Nestled along the banks of the Douro River, Aquapura is a stately terra-cotta-colored nineteenth-century fifty-room manor house with an Asian-themed interior that mixes candles with natural light and wood finishes. I would relax with aromatherapy massages, swims in the indoor pool, and other treatments that incorporated locally grown organic crops, such as grapes, olives, and cherries. The experience warmed my soul, and I did not want to leave the healing embrace of Aquapura.

During this time, so many of my friends stood by the wounded me. Letters and emails sent in for support were endless, from Lee, my longtime hairdresser and the bestest friend a girl could ever wish for, to Helen Jones, my personal assistant, who to this day gave the last drop of herself to me. I shall always honor the love and loyalty of my friends. People tend to think that they have to fix wounds by taking a pill or tumbling into destructive addictions. The cure lies in the support of friends and family who remain by your side in the darkest of hours.

A friend gave me this bit of wisdom, "Tall trees carry a lot of wind. Be the tall tree."

I would try . . . oh, how I would try.

From: David
To: Sarah
First, you might find it soulful to read St. Augustine's Confessions. He did things much worse, and because of it, was sainted! It is a beautiful book and will calm you down. Second, you must put the whole thing in perspective; you didn't do anything criminal, and millions of respectable people go round as their main career asking for money

for introductions! It's a totally legit thing to do in business. The entire concept of commissions is based on introductions! So you must not feel guilt-ridden. You committed an indiscretion, yes, but not much else.

Anyway, it is all past and undoable. If you dwell on your mistake, you will only commit another one. Stop soul-searching!

From: Sarah
To: David
My dearest,
Your naive and ignorantly stupid friend is trying to get a fresh canvas and a new pot of paints ready. Your steadfastness in friendship is heroic and I am in deep, deep honor and gratitude.

Love you,
Your Oriental sister, Moon

5 | *Montecito*

Find the lesson in what goes wrong.

A DEAR FRIEND IN California was gracious enough to provide me a home for two weeks in Montecito, a lovely community on the southern flank of Santa Barbara and wedged between the Santa Ynez Mountains and the Pacific. There I would attempt to calm the rough waters of my mind and soul. I needed to stop ruminating about who was going to sell me out next, which tabloid would want a chunk of me, and the self-doubt that had turned dark and brooding.

There are people who walk quietly into our lives and influence us simply by being themselves. Anamika, my friend and spiritual counselor, is such a person. She is a combination of gentleness, intelligence, and generosity that speaks to my heart. And, for reasons beyond my understanding, she came into my world and saw something in me that very few others had ever seen. I have been working with her for several years. She never gave up on me, even though I had essentially abandoned myself.

You might say, well, if I was doing all this work, how could I have made this terrible mistake? As Anamika always reminds me: It is about progress, not perfection.

I've always been hungry to examine myself, peel back my layers, and find the true Sarah, and so much work began.

Anamika and I decided that I needed to take some reflective time in Montecito to look at what had happened and how I could use it productively. "This is a wonderful opportunity; it gives us a chance to look more deeply," she said.

I had let my ego get in the way—again. The ego is that invisible barrier, that formidable enemy, we encounter every minute. Subtly, silently, it works—distracting our attention, diluting our reasoning, eventually destroying our judgment. The ego is sometimes completely innocuous, prodding us to hanker for affirmation, crave love and attention, or mercilessly blame ourselves. But each time, the ego has us in its grip.

Today the ego feels like a metal mask around my brain and head, I wrote in my diary. *It caused a buzzing in my ears. I started to get so angry and wished it would go away. I longed for the calm stillness I know I can feel, now that I am on the truth road. But I was getting angrier by the minute. Then, eventually, I realized that I should make friends with my ego. Accept it. Fill it with compassion and understanding. I realize it is important to take the higher*

*ground with my ego, not fight it, and in doing so, it eases, and a sense
of harmony ensues. A breakthrough, but it left me fairly worn out.*

In our sessions together, Anamika taught me that I didn't nec-
essarily want to get rid of the ego patterns driving the bus of my
life. I just shouldn't empower them. "Give the keys to your wiser,
empowered self," she counseled.

To do that, I had to feel—not "fix"—the impact of my ego
on my being. "If you are trying to fix or get something right, it
means that there is something wrong with you. If there is something wrong with you, then you are back in the loop of punishment
and judgment and that is what de-energizes our system. It literally
shuts us down," she told me.

"Whenever you say you're not valuable or you are a bad person or you are fat or ugly, you're turning your own energy against
yourself. You're punishing yourself to avoid being punished by
others. And you rob yourself of your inner resource, which is that
you are loved, loving, and loveable."

I tucked my knees up into my chest and wrapped my arms
around them, as if to shield myself from the world.

"I feel like such a failure."

"You are not a failure," she said.

"What do you think of me?" The words skidded out before I
had time to catch them.

"Well," Anamika said gently, "your real self is tender, gentle,
creative, and funny. You're a beautiful human being, you have a
future, you have value, you're the way you're supposed to be."

"I'm just so afraid I'm going to get it wrong, again."

"Sarah," she told me, "there is no wrong. There is a greater part
of you that is full of love and that you can access."

But how?

Anamika had me literally take a deep breath and move my focus from my head down into my body, traveling systematically through the body, stopping at each part to experience whatever sensation was present. This work shifted me from a thinking mode to a feeling mode that would include emotions and sensations of energy. How did I feel when punishing myself? How did I feel when blaming myself? How did I feel when I verbally beat myself up?

Ouch.

I saw how physical sensations result in either pleasant or unpleasant feelings and how I tend to react to this pleasantness or unpleasantness in habitual ways. With this exercise there was no attempt to replace the "bad" attitudes toward the self with the "good" attitudes toward the self. Instead, I witnessed the judgments, criticisms, and impatience. I saw how they made me suffer emotionally and created restlessness and agitation in my body. I got to know the nature of my hindrances by experiencing their horrid effects on me.

Ironically, there were days in Montecito when I missed Royal Lodge, and I shared my longing with Anamika. What I do love—no, let's call it a passion—about Royal Lodge is the bluebell woodland that surrounds it in the spring. Perhaps it's due to vivid childhood memories of playing and picnicking on an endless carpet of bluebells in the woods near my home in Dummer, I don't know.

Bluebells bloom in the first steady warmth of April and May. They flood the woods with a sea of lavender-blue flowers and a sweet, lingering aroma that magically banishes all memory of winter. Wood or wild hyacinth, as the plant is also known, favors the dappled sunlight and humus-rich soil found beneath the deciduous trees that rim the forest's edge.

Britain is also home to more bluebells than any other country. There's a certain irony that one of the least wooded countries in Europe is the international stronghold of this iconic woodland flower, but the reasons for its proliferation have as much to do with Britain's climate as the amount of suitable woodland.

Sometimes you see just one bluebell, an outlier poking up from opportunistic weeds, but usually the bluebells travel in packs. Some may be past their best, others bent or broken. But no matter, they form the most beautiful patches along a trail, and there are places where they ramble across the landscape and turn the woods into a Bluebell Kingdom.

On warm days, when the blue sky of spring is smiling down and the gentle breeze playfully sways the trees, I like to rise in the early morning when no one else is up. I walk slowly through the woods, where a sea of blue squeaks under my feet. On a single walk in springtime I can often count up to thirty different kinds of wildflowers in bloom, peeking out from the bluebells. There are many birds flying all around, chirping and fluttering their wings. They seem to be excited, and I know the touch of spring has brightened their day. To me the bluebell woods is a place of great tranquility and freedom. It gives me peace and restores my soul.

If I can't go to the bluebell woods in person, then I go there in my mind. Meditating on the bluebells brings greater peace into my life, as well as a refreshing and lasting sense of clarity and security. It is a way for me to escape the world around me and to put aside my worries. It is a place inside me where I feel warm, whole, loving, caring, in touch with the real me. My bluebell wood is my sacred inner place that no one can penetrate or pollute. It is where I go, when I go.

During my sojourn in Montecito, I wrote frequently in my diary.

DIARY ENTRIES

July 2, 2010

Today I chose thankfulness and forgiveness. I am thankful to Sarah, warts and all. Not that I actually have warts! I did find it difficult to forgive myself, but I am grateful for all the good bits and bad bits as they have got me here. I have detached from the constant brain chatter, and see it as only stories I tell myself, not reality. I caused so much pain and hurt to my family and myself, and the trail of debts and chaos that I have left behind. What a cleanup, and I feel sorry for Andrew, having to clean it up.

July 3, 2010

My two-week stay in Montecito is coming to an end. I have made many friends here. Their kindness has been the beginning of my rebuilding. Yet today I hit a brick wall, headfirst. I felt paralyzed and hopeless and unworthy. I languished in it and I felt forlorn, miserable, and downright bolshie. After twenty minutes, I detached from the feeling—Anamika helps—turned to the kind Sarah inside, got my energy back, and went for a jog. I felt so much better, especially since I am learning how to detach from my thoughts of so much self-doubt.

July 4, 2010

I played a Whitney Houston CD and listened to a track called "I Didn't Know My Own Strength." The words are so right: "I tumbled but I did not crumble." Listening to this powerful song, I pulled my shoulders back, lifted my head high, and remembered the words of a refugee friend in Sierra Leone: "They can take my country, but not my soul."

July 11, 2010

All those noisy voices. The dark voices. When fear enters you, it is like a sinister person approaching the gates. Seeing no one at home, he enters and makes himself at home. In fact, he makes himself the landlord and puts everything in the house at his disposal. I have been trying all day to kick the unwanted landlord out.

I was diligent in my inner work, and, over the two weeks, something began to shift. Hindrances began to dissolve because I was not empowering them any longer. As they faded, their opposites—love, patience, self-acceptance, and nonjudgmental attitudes—arose in their place. In fact, I realized that I created more suffering for myself by trying to push away undesirable states or by clinging to those that were comfortable.

By the end of the two weeks, I felt more at peace with myself. My chin was up. My attitude was hopeful. I felt like the tall tree.

NUGGETS:

• Detox yourself. Enjoy a drink of grated ginger root and hot water. Try watercress soup, or try the watercress soup diet, which is a seven-day detox.
• Sit quietly and notice your breaths and your heartbeat, rather than any racing thoughts. Anytime you catch yourself saying something negative—like "I look fat and ugly"—stop and take three deep breaths. Feel those breaths and listen to your heart.

- Go for a fast walk or run. This gets feel-good endorphins going in your brain and stops you from sitting down and mulling over bad thoughts or feeling sorry for yourself.

From: Charlie

To: Sarah

Try to be within yourself for some time. Discover what is beautiful about you. For the moment it is what it is. You are a fantastic human being. And forget all the others. Your generosity will win. The best gift of all is your nature. Think positive.

From: Leonora

To: Sarah

Dear sweet soul,

Always choose peace above all the commotion that surrounds you in daily life. We are only witnesses to the drama that unfolds. Mostly we are here in our human bodies to realize who we are and, as you well know, we are none other than God having an experience of Him, Her, It, Self.

I am always holding you in loving prayer. I pray that you have had time to delve into your true being which is none other than God's beautiful creation. All we go through in life is a series of experiences. It's what we learn from them that is important. You, my dear, have been through so much in your life that I hope you are choosing peace, where nothing and no one can harm you.

To: Robin and Scott

From: Sarah

Dear lovely Robin and Scott,

I am sorry for my foolishness. Andrew and the girls are amazing and they all know the truth. However bad the press is, we know. I guess it took this to strip me away to nothing, to stop the 25 years of being the Duchess. I am now Sarah. Just Sarah.

I have been on a spiritual retreat for 3 weeks now, and have been trying to rebuild myself from within.

It appears that the great mother I am to my children, I should have been to myself.

Much love and gratitude.
Sarah
Xxxx

From: Beatrice
To: Mummy York
Dear Mummy,
This is so strange, not speaking to you for this length of time. It is so weird. We are so missing you, Mummy, that we cannot wait till Spain when we can laugh and play and have fun and enjoy our little world and many adventures. This week is going well. Granny is in very good form. Eugenie and I are helping her with her little bits. We even had a picnic yesterday.

I've finished three books already. Yesterday, Eugenie went fishing and caught 54 mackerel. She had some for breakfast, and they tasted horrible.

We are so proud of you, Mummy, for doing all your stuff, looking beautiful, and kicking butts in LA. We know all this will mean so many exciting moments for the future and many adventures together to be had. We love you so much and cannot wait to see you.

DIARY ENTRY

July 6, 2010

You never know where you'll find a kind face, or pick up a bit of encouragement. I went through security at LAX, and a kind officer said to me, "My name is Morgan, and I am from Wales. And I say every day that it is our moral duty to be happy. It does not matter what messes we make, just clean them up and move on, having learned from them." I said I would always remember his kind smile and lovely words.

6 | *Lifeline*

Life is the sum of all decisions and choices
we've made so far.

*O*H, THE MIND, how it paints such a terrifying painting. And then you believe it. You find yourself sitting for hours
mulling the mind's masterpiece. With such thoughts invading my
mind, I felt it was time for penance. I have been known to wallow
in a paralyzing guilt that keeps me from doing anything useful.

What if I did something symbolic like they used to do in the
Old Testament days—like dress in sackcloth, smear myself with
ashes, and hit myself with a knout?

These were all acts of penance dating back to Biblical times and the early days of the Christian church. Parishioners dressed in an uncomfortable, hairy fabric, poured ashes on their heads, whipped themselves, and asked God to absolve them of their sins.

I did this in my mind. You might recoil at the idea of such self-abuse, even if only imaginary, but, you see, I felt I had made such a blunder of my life. I was so desperate to atone for my mistakes.

One of the greatest gifts in life is friendship. After the setup in May, Oprah gave me a hand of friendship and then introduced me to Martha Beck, who became one of the greatest life coaches one could have, and a dear friend. One of my "adopted" sisters, whose family I love and who I call Sisi, is Lisa Marie Presley. After my visit to Montecito, I bought a $700 round-trip ticket and set sail alone for her house in Hawaii. I felt really sorry for Lisa Marie. She put me in her best guest room. One morning, I broke the coffee machine because I neglected to use the filter papers! Then I nearly put my teacup with its silver-paint trim into the microwave.

As I sat down for coffee, I wrestled with my ego by thinking what could go wrong in my future. Could I go to jail? And if so, what would I be going for? Did I do something in my desperation that will return to bite me?

To tame my crazy thoughts, I went for a run. I looked for a shoreline to run on, but got lost and found myself vaulting over a locked gate into someone's garden. Then I ended up on the ninth hole of a golf course where I had to duck a swerving ball.

I spied a man in a green T-shirt and khaki shorts. He looked like he knew where he was going. I asked for directions and we struck up a conversation. He was Jeff from Nashville, the owner of a company that believes in rebranding (which was exactly what I needed), and was in Hawaii for an advertising conference. We chatted, and I asked him if he thought my business interests were beyond saving. Jeff explained to me that all companies these days were talking about enhancing their corporate image and self-esteem. There was hope for me yet! (Jeff had no idea where he was going on the Hawaiian shoreline either.)

It just so happened that Oprah and Lisa Marie had lunch the day before I arrived in Hawaii. They conspired together, and the next thing I knew I was whizzing my way to Oprah's home in Maui. We spent some delightful time with her. Her doggies and I chased each other up and down hills. Oprah and I became fast friends.

Some nights I talked for quite a while to the photos of my daughters, but they knew and I knew it was important to heal. I needed this time far from the madding crowd.

After my Hawaii interlude, I was reunited with Eugenie, Beatrice, and Dave Clark, Beatrice's fabulous boyfriend. We were invited to stay with some other friends, keen to offer their support to a friend in need.

To reach my friends, I boarded a small motorboat. From a distance I saw my girls. The island appeared a lush bump on a turquoise sea. As the boat bounced over slightly choppy waters, torrential rain pelted me, the wind whipped my hair, and the ocean spray spit up over the bow. I was sure I would look as if I had swum there, with giant flippers and frizzy hair. But I would feel safe, at home, in the arms of people who love me.

The girls were waiting for me on the dock, and all three of us cried with relief to be together again after a month. They helped me unpack and asked me to tell them of my adventures.

That night I wrote in my diary: *I enjoyed this present, the present of my daughters, the present of God's love, and the present of my giant mistake, which enabled me to see and appreciate all the gifts in my life. I am truly blessed.*

Yet sometimes the best of spirits can be dampened, if we let it happen. While I walked with Beatrice and Eugenie and watched them learn how to kitesurf, the media was mocking me again. In June, I had to lay off some of my staff due to mounting financial problems. The media aimed their torpedoes straight at me, criticizing me for jetting off abroad after letting my staff go. But being out of the United Kingdom was the safest place for my mind. However, the media would never understand this, even though I was staying with friends as their guest. Again, I had to bear the strain and get on with it, just as my father taught me. I held my head high, with elegance and grace. I hoped to change the negative energy swirling around me.

After rereading my words, I realize it might appear as if I were on one long lavish trip, but it really was the huge generosity of great friends who happen to live in exquisite places and were my gateposts when the tornado hit. Dorothy and Toto held on tight and so did I.

I traveled to Málaga, a lovely harborside city on the southern coast of Spain. I stayed with a dear friend of my mother's, Edwina, who had named her son Hector after my Argentine stepfather. Hector is my godson.

I was given young Hector's room (Hector was eighteen). As I looked around, I saw a photo of my mum, cradling newborn Hector in her arms, and looking at me and smiling. I smiled back at her beautiful face and felt her presence all around me.

There was also a photo of Hector, my stepfather, on the wall.

The room had the soothing smell of polo and horses, wafting from Hector's polo boots, which were slung in the corner, as if he would appear any moment to put them on. Suddenly I felt as if I were back in the old life I once knew with Mum and Hector, with its wonderful culture and sublime ways. Back then I had no reputation and I could simply be myself.

I saw Michelle, my lovely lady who has looked after me and my family for more than nine years while we are in Spain. She greeted me with her usual loving embrace and mischievous smile. She radiates positivity—it is infectious—and shows the purity of a golden loving heart. I saw tears in her eyes; she read my heart. "We can do this together. I know you and love you," she said gently.

Despite her words, I felt inadequate because I had let her down. She was one among so many others.

At bedtime, I put on my pink pajamas. They made me look like an uncooked sausage. I hoped that young Hector would not jump into his bed, forgetting that his jet-lagged godmother would be snoring loudly in the boiling heat of a non-air-conditioned room.

Before drifting off to sleep, I scribbled furiously in my diary: *How could I have dishonored myself and made so many people call into question their loyalty, love, and friendship for me? What they saw on that diabolical day, May 23, was not who they knew and loved. How could they possibly love Fergie for behaving in such a way? I feel I have let so many down. My self-hatred and self-punishment is rampant. I cannot forgive myself. I need healing.*

The British press once again plastered me all over the front pages, claiming that I was bankrupt with five million dollars in debt. It was a serious leak; someone had fed the press every ounce of my life.

With negativity comes great positivity. I wrote to a friend who understands the brutality of the press: *I am following your instructions and not going to give energy to these snakes, but I have to feel it is all for a reason. I have decided that if I change within, the outside will reflect it. So I shall give that a shot. If the vilifying stops, I know I have found the solution—a superb example for the world to see. I compare this to a lightbulb that cannot shine without the right connections within. You need positive and negative to make the lightbulb shine!*

I was asked to do *Celebrity Master Chef* in Australia. I sent the email to Oprah and asked if she could please advise me if I should go to Australia to learn to cook. She said, "If you do any TV, do a docuseries for the OWN network. I haven't asked if you would do this because you are my friend and I don't mix business with pleasure, but will you think about it?" And I did think. I was so very touched and that's how I decided to do the docuseries *Finding Sarah*, in which I would share with viewers my personal struggle to rebuild my life—and in doing so, help other people. It would be a six-part series, in which I would work with experts like Dr. Phil McGraw, Suze Orman, and Martha Beck to rebuild my life.

I couldn't believe it. I looked at it cosmically: Here I was in retreat, doing the positive spiritual work of connecting with my greater self, feeling more at peace with who I am—and this opportunity presented itself.

Was it luck? Was it coincidence? Was it a mystical force, some unknown and unpredictable phenomenon? Was it God? What was it?

To me, it meant that we must be prepared for blessings, but blessings come in their own good time. They await the right time, the right attitude, and the right opportunity to surface.

Doing the docuseries would be one thing. But truly finding

myself would be another. There was so much more work ahead. And I asked my friends for any prayers they could spare.

From: Sarah

To: Paddy and Sarah T.

My dearest Paddy and Sarah,

After the last disastrous scenario, I stopped the treadmill, and got off the busy world of life. I know you will be happy for me that I have done this, what a shame it had to be such foolishness that stopped my old life. I took myself away, a long way away ... And I am working hard on Sarah. I am trying to forgive myself for hurting so many people, mainly myself.

We all make mistakes, but this one has caused me to face my whole life.

Andrew and the girls are here for me, of course. But I have to be there/here for myself.

I pray one day the old Ferg will return.

All my love,

Fergo

From: Beatrice

To: Sarah's Diary

Hello, diary. I was worried a little through all this learning, Mummy would be different somehow and I would have missed something on her journey that I am so desperate to share and learn from. I was so relieved to be back with my mum, but even more exciting, she is coming back to be the mum I know—the super mum.

DIARY ENTRY

July 22, 2010

Well, it seems like we are a few days off bankruptcy, but my Ex is working flat out to help me. Bless him.

It will be good to be free, but I am struggling with the emotional damage left in the wake. I love the unity of my family. Now that is magic.

I cannot get over the miracle of being offered the docu-series. It will be amazing. It is all magic.

7 | *Return to Dummer*

When you begin to wake up and realize that the life you thought you lived in is not real at all, and that you can really choose the energy of goodness and calmness, it is there for you.

*I*N AUGUST 2010, I returned to my life in the UK, such as it was. It is strange to love the country you live in, but not be able to live there. After being gone for a while, I felt renewed, with a soul mostly cleansed of desperation and fear, and I was beginning to like the new me. Being back was something akin to rewatching a favorite movie that no longer thrilled me. But the movie hadn't

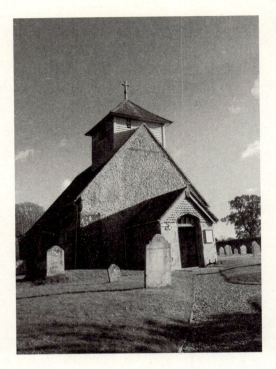

changed; I had. Yet, back in London, I always had a gnawing sense in my heart that my new feelings weren't real and that at any minute everything could come tumbling down.

I was there with my daughters to attend the wedding of my half sister Alice Ferguson in Dummer, where I grew up. Alice, who had been a bridesmaid at my own wedding in 1986, was marrying banker Nick Stileman of Singapore.

This was the first time I had been back to Dummer Down since my father died in 2003. My stepmother, Sue, lived on there after Dad's death. Before the wedding, I spent time walking around the house and grounds, remembering my childhood. It is so special and beautiful. There are tall lime trees growing all around, and lavender bushes with white roses threading through them.

I saw Michael Borlase, our farm manager. He has been in our family for forty years. We reminisced about my childhood when I wore my Wellington boots under my very smart party dress, so that I could pat my ponies on the way to the parties. All the old staff hugged me and said no matter what, they would always stand firm in loving me. I cried over their goodness and care.

As I walked around the house, I experienced a form of time travel: the house smelled exactly as it did when I was a little girl, a particular kind of musty warmth; the lemony, ubiquitous scent of just-laundered clothes; and delightful aromas wafting from the country kitchen.

The experience engulfed me in waves of nostalgia. Home. It is where the heart is. (So they say.) It is sausages cooking in the kitchen and childhood memories—the place that shaped you, the place you return to on holidays to find family and friends.

Many hate the idea of visiting a previous residence and discovering that the backdrops of their memories have been altered, but I love the little jolts of recognition . . . the old oil-fueled stove . . . the spot where the dog bowl used to be . . . the scrubbed pine table in the kitchen . . . These fragments of time popped into my head like the name of a forgotten classmate. It was comforting to see that traces of my occupancy had somehow outlasted almost forty years. Every surviving detail was a pushpin holding the past to the wall.

The service was shared by a special gathering of family and friends, held at Dummer's All Saints Church. All Saints Church, Dummer, is recorded in the Domesday Book of 1086. The oldest visible part of the present building is the south doorway of the

This is my brother, Andrew, driving our old gray
Massey-Ferguson tractor, taking
Alice and Nick away from the church.

nave—which dates from the twelfth century. The pulpit is one of the oldest pulpits in the country, constructed about 1380 in the Perpendicular style.

The flag overhanging the nave from the seventeenth-century balustrade of the gallery is a Sovereign's Standard of the Life Guards, laid up here after Queen Elizabeth II presented the regiment with a new standard. The battle honors borne on the flag range from Dettingen (1743) and Waterloo (1815) to Ypres and the Somme, between 1914 and 1918. The standard was given to the church by the late colonel Andrew Ferguson—my grandfather, who was a commanding officer of the regiment and who held the office of church warden here for several years.

Jane Austen (1775–1817) lived in nearby Steventon for twenty-five years; her father was the rector of the thirteenth-century church of St. Nicholas. In all probability, Jane attended her friends' weddings here at All Saints in Dummer.

The bells of this small village church have been rung in Dummer for more than four hundred years. The oldest bell in the peal of five was cast in 1590, while the newest was installed to celebrate the coronation of King George V in 1911.

Alice, who is a modelesque gorgeous blonde anyway, looked even more stunning in her beautiful big white gown with a lace shrug and carried a hand-tied bouquet of white roses. Alice and Nick left the ceremony in an old trailer and tractor, adorned with flowers.

As I watched the happy couple, I prayed in my heart that Alice would never have to go through the learning curve of life as I have had to do. I hoped she would come to terms with the feelings in her heart and soul and not have to learn them by being totally humiliated.

Friends my age—I am fifty-one—tell me that they, too, often find themselves caught up in the details of their childhood, but I wonder if they ever find, as I do, that going home again brings a tinge of loss, of seeing who we were in our innocence, and our youth being gone, replaced with a harder, often scarred maturity.

As we parted ways, we all hugged good-bye. "Take care of yourself," said Sue. "You're the best."

Dummer will always be a part of who I am, what I feel, and how I look at life—part of my scrapbook of life. In a way, we all can go home again. In fact, it can be a very important part of moving forward.

DIARY ENTRY

> August 13, 2010
> *Phew . . . we signed with OWN last night. We start to roll . . .*
> *A whole new start. I am so grateful.*
> *And now I must further reflect . . . I have a desperate fear of abandonment and a need for constant reassurance. I guess this goes back to my mum leaving so hastily for Argentina, and seeing her in such pain and anguish for so many years, and I could not fix her.*
> *I felt her absence from me so profoundly. I felt her own suffering, losing Hector at age 50 to cancer. All so tragic.*
> *I must have turned into a people-pleaser at age 10. I wanted desperately to do anything to lift Mum's sadness.*
> *I fear if I am not perfect, everyone will leave. I know this is not real, but it lives in my tormented, troubled darkness.*

8 | *Sister Act*

Tell the ones you love that you love them whenever you can.

$\mathcal{W}$HEN I WAS eight years old, my sister Jane used to pick the heads off roses and put them in my pocket, then tell Mum I had done it. As children, we would fight so much, and Jane loved nothing more than getting me to lose my redheaded temper. One time, I lashed out and poked her with a pencil. To this day, she carries a piece of that lead pencil lodged in her hand.

A little exasperating, a little sweet, but always the perfect shoulder to lean on. Here's what sisters do for you: They provide you with a reality check. They are the ones who tell you when you have lipstick on your teeth, or when you look fat in a dress, or when you're being an idiot. They tell you the truth because you need to hear it, but it doesn't alter the bond between you. And they are ready to take on the world for you and know you inside out.

I look at pictures of Jane throughout our lives. I see a beautiful, delicate-looking English girl with high cheekbones, long colt legs, beaming brown eyes, and a lovely slim tapered figure. Someone familiar with our family might mistake her for our mum.

As I mentioned earlier, when I was sixteen, Jane disappeared from my life: She married Australian farmer Alex Makim on July 26, 1976. Our father did not approve at all. We later found out that he had written a letter to Alex's father, which said, "My daughter goes to Australia not with my support, but with my cooperation." It was a gentlemanly letter; he was trying to protect Jane. He had already spoken to Alex and told him they were doing the wrong thing. At one point, Dad tried to stall the blossoming love affair by sending Jane on a seven-month trip to Africa. But the separation only made the couple's feelings stronger.

After Jane returned to London, Alex met her and proposed. Dad, who had finally mellowed over the romance, hosted a wedding reception for Jane and Alex at home. Mum came, of course, and everything was fine until the party was over and those two women I loved so much had gone. Jane's marriage took her from our rural English home to Australia's tough outback.

In Jane's new country, there was no hired help. She did everything, mustering cattle on horseback, driving a tractor, farming, branding, cooking, and cleaning. There was no phone and the only way that Jane could keep in touch with her family back home was by using a primitive Morse code device, which she dubbed "the party line." At times she was engulfed by homesickness, but she refused to cave in and kept herself busy. Of course, for Jane, life in Australia was very much a romantic dream. It taught her much about resilience and survival and had a great deal to do with the person she is today.

Jane lived in the outback for thirteen years and had two children with Alex: Seamus, now a cameraman based in the Canary Islands, and Ayesha, a former model who teaches English to Japanese students.

During those years, Jane traumatically lost four babies at different stages of pregnancy, and each time was as hard as ever. Four babies died, at four and a half, five, and five and a half months. She was once forced to carry a baby that had died inside her womb. She was sent home from the hospital to "let nature take its course," but it didn't, and after three weeks of hell carrying a dead baby boy, she begged the doctors to take it out.

The fourth was born alive at eight and a half months, but died of a rare disease. Jane held the infant, a baby girl, in her arms, while being told that the child would not live that long. The baby was wrapped in a soft blanket and crowned with a tiny pink cap—beautiful to behold. The nurses let Jane cradle her for as long as she wanted. Someone in the hospital asked her what she wanted to name the baby and what kind of coffin she wanted. As you might imagine, Jane was traumatized by the experience, and it will never leave her.

Jane's marriage to Alex started to go sideways and she separated from him in 1989. They became embroiled in a bitter custody dispute, which he won. The judge ruled that the children would be better protected on the farm than with their mother in Sydney because of all the media attention. Worse still, when Jane attempted to visit Seamus and Ayesha, she found them locked inside the farm gates, fearful that they'd be kidnapped.

Jane remarried in 1994. Her husband was German-born Rainer Luedecke, a marketing consultant with whom she has a daughter, Heidi, age fifteen, who is at school in Sydney. She is a budding artist, and I bet that with her enormous heart and spirituality, she will become a leader of goodness. Jane and Rainer's marriage lasted nine years.

Jane went on to become a successful public relations consultant in Sydney. Her efficiency in business, however, never undermined her maternal commitment. In fact, if you asked either of us what was the most important thing we've done in our lives, we'd both say, "Having children."

We are devoted to each other's children. I remember the time when Eugenie underwent an operation to have steel rods inserted into her spine. Doctors told me that my daughter could have ended up in a wheelchair had they not operated. I was shocked and scared. Few outside our family knew that the operation was more serious than a heart bypass or that the surgery, which was supposed to take two and a half hours, ended up taking more than eight hours. I stayed by my daughter's bedside for nine days and nine nights. Jane stayed strong for both me and our father, who was also ill in the hospital. She went from one hospital to the other.

I sometimes wish that Jane would tell me what toll my life has taken on her, but she does not. I know, however, that Jane has been forced to live, often uneasily and warily, in the harsh reflected glare of my endless torrent of criticism and scandal. At times, people turned their backs on her, and she began to lose all her work. Imagine how hard this would be for someone like Jane who works in the people business of public relations and communications. Today, thankfully, Jane is the sponsorship manager of St. Vincent's Hospital in Sydney.

Jane fights on for me. In 2010, a magazine plastered this headline on its cover: "Fergie Sleeps with 3 Sheikhs for $500,000 on a Boat in the Mediterranean." Jane led the charge to take this case to the most famous litigation attorney in Sydney. To our utter dismay, he told us there was nothing we could do, because they had more money and wanted more than anything to get me into the courtroom. We had to limp away from the lawyer, knowing that, yet again, I was accused of something I did not do, with no means to retaliate.

Just as the bird depends on the shelter of its nest, we find protection in the love and support of our family. Jane has been one of my staunchest defenders, particularly when she met me in Los Angeles after the Fake Sheikh scandal. She will often launch into a passionate outburst on my behalf. She once told a reporter, "Sarah does an awful lot, but you only hear about the bad things that she does. Sarah doesn't get recognized for all the good things she does. She has a wonderful heart and will help anyone. She probably does far too much for other people and doesn't look after herself. She exhausts herself."

Jane and I are quite different in personality. She's capable; I'm funny . . . except for when I'm surprisingly capable, and she's inexplicably funny! When Jane becomes emotional and holds back tears, her top lip twitches. When she laughs, she throws her humble kind heart into every cackle, and her enthusiasm is childlike in every way. Jane stills sees life as magic.

Both Jane and I are grateful for our stepmother, who gave our family a brother, Andrew, and two more beautiful sisters, Alice and Eliza. We adore them so much and are proud of everything they

have accomplished in their lives. If there is such a thing as a perfect family, we have it, and I miss them all.

Friends are wonderful, but there is nothing that can replace the feeling of being with your sister. Alice Walker was right when she said, "Is solace anywhere more comforting than that in the arms of a sister?"

No, it is not. She is your best friend, one that you can never get rid of. You can get mad at her or love her and even take her for granted, but she is always going to be there for you, forever.

NUGGETS:

- Blockages in relationships thicken when you refuse to release being right. Like an egg, the longer your refusal boils, the harder you get.
- Today, approach a loved one with whom you've argued and

apologize if you were wrong. And if they were wrong, then also apologize. Pouncing on your pride is a greater sign of strength than pounding on your chest.

- Don't let time or distance keep you from your loved ones.
- Whenever you can, tell the ones you love that you love them.
- Never let the sun go down on an argument. Always take the high ground of any argument, and having said your piece, practice the three Cs: Communication, Compromise, and Compassion.
- Always be grateful for your family and friends.

From: Jane
To: Sarah
Darling Stinks, with my love xxx
Praise and Blame—Buddha:

This has been going on through the ages:
They criticize the silent ones.
They criticize the talkative ones.
They criticize the moderate ones.
There is no one in the world who escapes criticism.
There never was and never will be,
Nor is there now,
The wholly criticized
Or the wholly approved.

There is absolutely no way to avoid being criticized. Nobody gets through life described as totally wonderful.

The question is: What do we do with criticism? Do we take it in, believe it, and develop self-loathing? Do we assume that a criticism of something we have done is a condemnation of who we are?

Or can we filter criticism and keep it focused as perhaps valuable but private information? Can we look for the kernels of truth that might help us improve? Can we not immediately push criticism away, yet not accept it totally?

And can we treat praise the same way, not instantly basking in our glory? Praise and shame are two sides of the same coin. If we are eager to accept praise, then we are equally vulnerable to feel the sting of blame.

In both cases, we need to listen with caution and discernment. There are truths in what people say about us, good and bad, but let's not ever believe that their words define us.

9 | *Looking for Love*

*The only problem I have is finding a man who
would put up with me and all that entails,
including the media interest.*

$\mathcal{T}$HE CROWD AT the party was three deep, aglow
with the light of candles in squat yellow holders dancing on shal-
low pools of melted wax. I was there with my handsome Ex, who
was my date, at the home of some very dear friends of ours in the
London countryside. Everyone was drinking and talking. A riff of
laughter rose from a nearby table. From across the room I spied
a glossily handsome man, stunningly so, like the head shot of a

film star. He must have been Italian, with his thick black hair and amused green eyes.

"Damn, Sarah, not you too!" broke in a girlfriend of mine who had apparently also noticed the handsome Italian. He and I made eyes at each other until I, in my black cocktail dress tied at the waist with fancy cord, finally got up the nerve to go talk to him—or, should I say, let him talk to me. If you're looking for a man, you've got to be a lady. If you're too direct, it changes the game. I've scared off potential boyfriends in the past with my headstrong personality, or because they think I'm too close to Prince Andrew. In a word, my love life has been "diabolical."

During our conversation, I learned he was recently divorced, which piqued my interest even more. I could feel the twinkle of those eyes and the intimacy of that private smile. Yet the longer we chatted, the more I could feel that nothing would come of it. There are things in life that are not meant to be. I just knew it in my heart of hearts. But it was fun to flirt.

I will tell you that in my heart there is truly an absence of romance, of having someone to love, love me back, and the intimacy. Yes, I do love Andrew deeply. When we were married, ours was a true love match. But why was love not enough?

Yes, it was love. It is now. I believe it was meant to be like this. I know I have to go my own path, because I am a free spirit. And he has to go his path. I think we both realize that we were very naive, but we loved each other very much. That's why the love is still there. We're growing again now. Our love bond is extremely strong—but in its right place for us.

Beatrice and Eugenie are certainly happy with the way things are. They always say, "No, we don't want you to get back together, because you get on so well." Andrew and I have brought them up, joint parenting, and we are so secure in our friendship that they know that and are safe with it. They have peace because we both are free to come and go. We are completely and utterly in harmony. I always say our relationship is similar to what Kahlil Gibran says in *The Prophet:* "And stand together yet not too near together: / For the pillars of the temple stand apart, / And the oak tree and cypress grow not in each other's shadow."

Andrew calls ours the happiest divorced family in the world. There are many reasons for this; all I can say is the highs and lows we've shared are proof that ex-husbands and wives can preserve what was right about their relationship. A mutual condition of our divorce was that we would share equally in parenting our girls. We may disagree occasionally, but by and large we have made a success of living together by being apart.

What of our separate lives? There are tough moments, to be sure. Since the collapse of our marriage, Andrew has dated a string of beautiful women. And, yes, I've felt jealous. I'm only human that way. I confess that I have never found anyone to replace Andrew in my affections.

Andrew is a great man and a thoroughly good person. He's a model boy. He doesn't drink, goes to bed early, and gets up at 8:30 AM. The girls and I have full admiration for him because he keeps such discipline. I'm the mischievous one. On weekends I'll stay in bed as long as I can.

My daughters and I are so close, yet it makes me realize how much I missed having a mother around as a young girl. Now is the time in my daughters' lives when they need to know their mother is strong and there. That's why I talk to my children about everything.

For the longest time Beatrice wanted a boyfriend. I told her she mustn't fret or worry if other people have boyfriends. Her time would come. One day she had a wobbly and said she didn't want to be grown up, not that day, so she just sat with me and had a hug. It's okay to be a little girl, I told her. I'm middle-aged and I still feel like a little girl.

When my girls lobbied to date and have boyfriends, I listened before expressing any reservations, and I shared their excitement at making an emotional connection with boys. I let them know that it's normal to have romantic and sexual feelings. I told them that things like kissing and cuddling and having a boyfriend are fun, but that they had to think first about what is best for them. Some girls feel that being romantic and physical is the only way to be with a boy. As I said to Beatrice and Eugenie, there's a very good reason why there's "friend" in the word "boyfriend." How you help your child handle that initial crush may help set patterns for romantic relationships throughout her life.

After a few not-quite-right boyfriends, Beatrice's luck finally turned in a big way when she met Dave Clark. If I were to describe an ideal boyfriend for Beatrice, it would be him. He's fun, support-ive, loving—and cute as can be, and so is Jack. He and Eugenie are in a relationship and exploring what it's like to have someone spe-cial. She met him on the slopes of Verbier, where we were helping Andrew celebrate his fiftieth birthday. Jack was holidaying with a group of friends. He and Eugenie started dating and the relation-ship became quite serious.

Not long ago, I watched Eugenie from my window as she frolicked with Jack. I suppose he is her first true love, and her hap-piness exuded through the windowpane. Eugenie still managed, in her beautiful way, to stop and extract herself from Jack's amorous clutches to pop upstairs to tell me that she loved me.

Eugenie turned twenty-one in March 2011. On the day of her

birthday, I traveled by train to Newcastle to take her out for a surprise lunch. Jack couldn't be there, so I brought him with me in the form of an image of his face on Eugenie's birthday cake.

As for finding love, I remain idealistic. Deep inside, I am a romantic. And I've had plenty of boyfriends, from racecar drivers to business tycoons to counts—many of whom caused me painful public embarrassment. Even so, I believe there is a special someone still out there for me. I really do. I believe the very instant I set eyes on him, I will know. Perhaps it is on this journey that I am freeing up space in my life to have a partner.

If you asked me what I look for in a man, I'd tell you this: Someone who is good-looking and easy on the eyes. Someone with a good sense of humor, who doesn't mind the cameras on me. Someone who believes in old-fashioned chivalry, is confident, sophisticated, intelligent, and athletic. Someone who is positive and supportive of my goals. Someone who has integrity, honesty, and is family oriented. Someone who is a friend, too, and who knows me better than I know myself. Someone I can't bear to be apart from. And, oh, he has to pass the test of our Caramels, our four little Norfolk terriers, and, of course, Andrew and the girls.

As I look over this list, the résumé of my perfect mate, I realize I have just described Andrew.

DIARY ENTRY

> July 25, 2010
> *I long to be 40 again. I wished I'd had Demi Moore around to ask how she managed to lure Ashton Kutcher.*
> *I am having massive surges of why had I let my marriage*

go, why had I failed at keeping the amazing love that Andrew and I had together?

I feel a barrage of abuse and self-punishment coming on. My inner voice screamed: You could never even get an Ashton Kutcher, even if you did know the secret code.

10 | *Mind Chatter*

*Life is full of experiences, positive and negative,
and learning comes from all of them.*

I HAD BEEN FIGHTING self-hatred so long that I could
fight no more. I treated myself like a piece of antique china that
might, at any moment, crumble into dust. I felt disembodied, hol-
lowed out, in some horrible way unreal to myself.

I looked fine from the outside, usually, a woman coming into
her life. I had just started a new production company, was part
of a worldwide network of children's charities, had friends in the

United States and wonderful family back home in London. But the life I really lived took place inside my head: It buzzed and hissed with ceaseless, vicious criticism.

I'd berate myself ceaselessly. Why can't I be tall, blond, and good-looking? Why am I so fat and revolting? Why, why, why?

I tried to quiet this roar by stacking up achievements—*if I get this book published, this new project, maybe people will get that I'm really okay*—and with fervent self-affirmations that I wrote down in my diary. This would work for a few hours, until something small—a slightly self-conscious exchange with someone, a memory of some imperfection—would undo it all, the self-hate roaring back into my brain and body. I felt hounded, overpowered, nearly unstitched by it.

The mind starts out like a brilliant, precious gemstone. But over a lifetime, that shiny gem gets dirty, dusty, coated over by conditioned thoughts and the experiences we have. We lose touch with our inner brilliance—the light of the inner self—and can't even remember that it's there. What I needed was to clean my mind and whatever was blocking my own inner light.

To begin that process, I would work with psychologist Dr. Phil McGraw. My hope was that I'd find out why my mistakes had turned me into such a bad-luck magnet—and what I could do about it. I knew that I could not live the rest of my life repeating the self-destructive patterns of the past.

I am not a stranger to therapy. Many years ago, one of my girls needed help. Beatrice was having trouble reading in first grade and all the signs pointed to dyslexia. Then testing confirmed it and we took all the right steps so she could deal with it. After finding out I was the mother of a child with learning disabilities, I spent a great deal of time getting up to speed on everything to do with dyslexia.

Interestingly, I, too, had difficulty learning letters and numbers as a child. I decided to read up on learning disabilities because little was known about them back when I was in primary school. I was astonished to discover that as a child I matched many of the criteria associated with two learning disabilities: dyscalculia, problems with math concepts and problems, and attention-deficit/hyperactivity disorder (ADHD), which is characterized by distractibility and difficulties with staying on task.

I had myself evaluated by experts who confirmed that I am ADHD and moderately impaired by dyscalculia. Why is this relevant to a fifty-one-year-old woman? It matters a lot, because one does not outgrow these conditions. Without proper intervention people develop their own coping systems, some of which may be effective and others not at all. I believe these issues have had a profound effect on me throughout my life.

It is a known fact that many adults with ADHD have difficulty managing time, money, people, and projects. Certainly I do. Dyscalculia can make it hard to measure and quantify ordinary things such as money and time. I used to be chronically late for appointments because I'd schedule too many without regard for how long each would take or the travel time from one meeting to the next. Money has always slipped through my fingers, and I now realize I've never had an internal gauge for how much I spent.

Now it was time to dig deeper into my problems, so I steeled myself to face Dr. Phil. A plain-spoken Texan who at six foot four still looks like the college football player he once was, he welcomed me in—"I'm Phil," he said simply, but it was more than that. There was a quality of sincerity and care in his presence that made me feel that he genuinely wanted to help me. Working with him, I knew, would be frightening and liberating in equal measure.

Sometimes I talked a blue streak about the virulent self-loathing that wouldn't leave me alone, not for a day, rarely even for an hour, and my futile efforts to stave it off with harder work and endless instructions to be nicer to myself. Not much gave me pleasure anymore; worse, I'd be in the midst of an ordinary conversation when my internal guard dogs would begin to howl and yap so frantically that I'd lose all sense of what to say next.

During one of our sessions, a shameful story tumbled out: how, as a child, I survived a traumatic and turbulent childhood growing up in Britain.

I told him how my mother used to spank me because I wouldn't sit on my portable potty or wouldn't eat. A little vein would pop up on my forehead—my mother called it "the sign of the devil."

"I'm going to beat the devil out of you," she'd say.

One time, when I was two, Mother had a luncheon of ladies all dressed very smartly. She tied me to the potty and a table leg to keep me on the potty. I pulled and dragged myself, potty and table still attached, through the French doors and into the dining room where the ladies were lunching.

"Mum! Can you get me off my potty now!" I screamed. The ladies gasped in disgust.

Dr. Phil furrowed his brows. "You realize that's not okay, to lash a kid to a table and potty chair, right?"

"Well, no wonder I'm so flawed."

Dr. Phil sat in silence for a moment, allowing me to digest the assumption buried in his simple question.

"Here's the deal," he began. "I believe that every one of us has a personal truth: the thing we believe about ourselves when no one else is looking. And we live our lives based on that truth: We generate the results that we believe we deserve. If you feel flawed, I guarantee you it's because that's what you believe you deserve. What is your personal truth?"

"I believe I caused my mother to leave."

He asked me to tell him about it, and out tumbled the story of how my mother left when I was only thirteen.

Dr. Phil shook his head. "Who does that? I mean, seriously, who does that? Who dumps their child to go off to Argentina with some polo player? Who does that? Your mother."

His comment got a rise out of me. Later I would write in my diary that I was glad my mum did leave, because it made me aware of how fabulous my own girls are and that I could never leave them or not be there for them.

I explained to Dr. Phil that my relationship with my father disintegrated soon after. Living at Dummer Down took its toll: My self-esteem sunk lower. My dear father was quite lost, and in his own despair, he'd lapse into saying things he didn't really mean, like telling me I was a "sheep's ass," that I looked like a clown, that I should grow up and stop acting silly. He thought he was being funny, a typical English sense of humor. I was disgusted with my life. So, I just shut up and never said a word, though I cried every night because I was inconsolable.

Dr. Phil reflected a moment, then added: "No wonder you beat up on yourself all the time."

He went on to explain that parents, good or bad, are pivotal people in their children's lives. When they yell, criticize, or embarrass their children, they leave a permanent mark on them.

"When parents fail to point out what makes them proud or why a child is special, they write on the slate of that child. As children, we internalize what's written on that slate. So, on some level you're thinking, 'I'm not good enough; I'm not worthy.'"

I couldn't look at him. I just stared into my lap, my breath coming faster and faster. "Yes," I finally said in a wobbly whisper, "that's what I've always said to myself."

In truth, so much strife had always been brewing on the home front that I felt like I had to fix everything because it was my fault. Here's the truth: I am the pathological fixer. I'm the one who glues the broken teacup back together. I'm the one who rescues stray animals. And I'm the one who thought she had to fix our broken home.

But when your fixing doesn't work, you start believing that if you'd just done this or that, you could have prevented the problems. There's a lot of guilt. Growing up, I was the one in the family who strived to create harmony. This pattern continued in my life.

"So, you were born with a job?" Dr. Phil asked.

"Yes, the Fixer. Be happy . . . be jolly . . . always be in good form. I twirled around my parents as gracefully as I could, charming them, soothing them, anything to prevent them from getting mad at me. But the horrible, damning thing was that I couldn't. I know what it feels like to think, if only I'd made my bed, if only I'd behaved, maybe they would have gotten along."

I still feel like the Fixer today. I might be allowed time off, but I can't seem to quit this job.

"Tell me how you lost your mother."

Another story spilled out. It was in 1998 on a Sunday night, I told him. I rang her up to see how she was doing. The conversation went a bit like this:

"Mum, tell me you love me." My mother was not an affectionate woman with my sister Jane and me.

"Don't be so stupid. You don't need to hear that. Of course I love you."

"No, no, no . . . just tell me you love me."

"Oh, love you."

She begged to get off the phone because she had to drive to the supermarket to buy a steak.

That very night, she was killed instantly when the car she was driving collided with a van, driven by the farmer next door, on a rural road. My mother was decapitated. The driver of the other car suffered a broken ankle.

When the accident happened, Beatrice and Eugenie were with me on summer holiday in Tuscany. At four in the morning, my assistant at the time, Hilly Bett, called me with the tragic news. Mum is gone? I could not get my head around the idea. I stood silently at my window until the first light when reality sank in. Mum and I had so many good years to come, I thought.

I was the first to arrive at the ranch where my mother had made her home with Hector. To my dismay I found that after Hector's long and painful death from cancer in 1990, Mum had been living on the verge of bankruptcy, too proud to ask for help. The electricity, gas, and telephone had been cut off at the farm and there was no hot water. On the kitchen table was a stack of unpaid bills.

My mum had promised Hector before he died that she would keep their beloved ranch going at all costs. But Argentina's rocky economy pushed up interest rates on loans, crops failed at her farms, and a pony-breeding business was hit by competition. Each month I had sent several thousand pounds to my mother, but I was unaware of the full extent of her financial struggle.

Alone, in the shadows, next to my mother's coffin, I waited many hours for Jane to arrive with her son Seamus.

Once Jane and Seamus joined me, the three of us talked over whether we should view the body. It was Seamus who made the right call. He was only seventeen but he said, "Remember how beautiful she was and not how she might look now." I'm so glad we followed his advice.

In my therapy session, a certain rhythm was developing, and I could have continued, but Dr. Phil interrupted. "You just told me about a horrifying, tragic end to your mother's life, and you told me about it as though you were ordering lunch."

I paused, not knowing how to respond. I suppose time had detached me from the emotions I did have when she was killed.

Dr. Phil pronounced me "emotionally bankrupt."

I wasn't following him. "What does it mean to be emotionally bankrupt?"

"You are depressed. You are anxious. You have self-hatred. You have a disconnect. You put up a wall. You unplug from people and you have an internal, emotional meltdown."

I didn't disagree with him. The very way I was handling things—upbraiding myself for every interaction, doubting every overture, withdrawing from the friends I did have—only ensured that I would keep loathing myself.

Dr. Phil continued. "You have had a lot of rejection in your life. You have had it from your mom; you have had it from your dad. The decisions you've made in your life that were really destructive were set in motion many, many years ago, just sleeping inside you for a place to wield their destruction.

"Your internal dialogue needs to change—that little voice inside you, that sometimes nagging voice that just won't shut up. You need to realize: 'I don't have to think this way anymore. It's not anyone else's fault that I am the way I am. I choose what I think, feel, and do, and that's a tremendous power. I have the power to choose who I am going to be and how I am going to live my life.'"

During this conversation, I confessed to him that when I look in the mirror, I tell myself that I'm so disgusting that it's no wonder no one loves me.

"Now, what would you think if one of your daughters looked in the mirror and said, 'You're disgusting'?"

I would feel deep pain if my daughters did that. But fortunately, they don't. At ages twenty and twenty-two, Beatrice and Eugenie are everything I hoped they would be as young women—beautiful, well-adjusted, kind, and giving—and they always make me immensely proud.

Dr. Phil said that once I changed my internal dialogue, I would heal my personal truth. We zeroed in on my negative thoughts about myself. He slowly convinced me that they were distortions. The relief was indescribable. I began to understand how my distorted thoughts were really the cause of my bad feelings, and ultimately, my destructive behavior.

If you're really going to change counterproductive patterns of behavior, you're probably going to need to change the way you speak to yourself. After all, what you say to yourself is usually an extension of your beliefs. We all talk to ourselves on a regular basis throughout the day, and this commentary typically revolves around the obstacles and opportunities we face. Yet people often don't realize that their inner voice is speaking; they simply accept what it has to say as the gospel truth. This is what Dr. Phil means by internal dialogue. What you tell yourself can have a profound effect, for better or worse, on how you feel, what you do, and how you see the world. Depending on the content of these internal messages, they can help or hinder your life—and your ability to reach your goals.

If you haven't liked yourself for a long time, you're used to saying negative things to yourself. Now you must shift and listen to a positive voice that can be found through self-exploration.

I don't have all the answers on how to do this, but I will tell you what I do. I turn to nature for peace of mind. I find a quiet place in nature and I sit still, slow down, and wait. When I slow down long enough, my thoughts seem to turn off on their own. I just look, listen, and the wonder always comes. Whether it's the sight of a hawk soaring above or birds picking at the bread crumbs I've put out for them, eventually something will touch that spot deep inside me that feels wonder and awe.

Become aware of your mind chatter, but don't try to chase it away. Instead, do what I call "sitting at the end of the bed." Perch at the end of the bed and pretend you're talking to Harvey, the white rabbit, from the play and movie of the same name.

Its central character, you may recall, is one Elwood P. Dowd, a congenial tippler whose best pal is the six-foot white rabbit, Harvey. No one else can see Harvey, and that's the rub. Elwood insists on introducing him to his sister's society friends, to fellow drinkers at the corner bar, to anyone, in fact, who crosses his meandering path. Harvey, he reasons, is such a delightful companion that others deserve to know him, too.

Like Elwood, we all have this ability to invent characters, so why not invent ones that can help with our thoughts and feelings and our desire to improve our lives? No, really. It can work. Our own inner talk is so full of demands, self-judgment, and play-by-play criticism. Try something new. Conjure up an imaginary friend (it doesn't have to be Harvey) who can talk to you in positive, nurturing, empowering ways. You'll notice that you will be able to replace your negative self-talk with conversations from your beloved imaginary entity. Just don't introduce him to your friends!

Finally, begin to view your obstacles as just chairs in your way. You can maneuver around them, put them in a different place, or even replace them. Obstacles are movable.

Dr. Phil has now become a pivotal person in my life—one of the finest, strongest, kindest gentle giants I have ever met. I owe such a debt of gratitude to him; he never left me alone while I was trying to find my way. My work with him reminds me of a story I recently saw on a video.

A blind beggar was sitting on the pavement. He held up a sign that said: I AM BLIND, PLEASE HELP. There were only a few coins in his begging bowl.

A lady walked by. She took a few coins from her purse and dropped them into the bowl. She then took the sign, turned it around, and wrote some words. She put the sign back so that everyone who walked by would see the new words.

Many more people started giving money to the blind man, and soon the bowl began to fill up.

That afternoon the lady who had changed the sign came to see how things were. The beggar recognized her footsteps and asked, "Were you the one who changed my sign this morning? What did you write?"

The lady said, "I wrote only the truth. I said what you said but in a different way."

What she had written was: TODAY IS A BEAUTIFUL DAY AND I CANNOT SEE IT.

Of course both signs told passersby the man was blind. But the first sign simply stated this fact. The second sign told people they were so lucky that they were not blind.

It is all in our words, and what we tell ourselves, whether we can see the things we like about ourselves and all the good in our lives, or not.

Dr Phil taught me how to see.

NUGGETS:

- We all feel the way we think. So change how you think if you want to change the way you feel.
- Turn to nature. If we want to keep ourselves at peace, we have to have a lovely, peaceful moment every day in nature. You will always catch yourself saying I haven't got time, and I say to you the only thing that will give you time is by making time.
- Become aware of your mind chatter. Sit at the end of the bed and talk to your imaginary friend. Rent the movie *Harvey*.
- See the obstacles in your life as chairs. You can move them around, or out of the way, at will. Or if they are in your way, climb over them. See yourself doing that in your mind; it will make you chuckle. A sense of humor always quiets the negativity in the mind.
- Accept that you cannot control every situation, past or present, and absolve yourself of unwarranted blame. If you do blame yourself—and you will—just remember that you're human. I always tell myself, "Duchess or no Duchess, I am always here to learn from my experiences."

DIARY ENTRY

July 16, 2010

When you begin to wake up and realize that the life you thought you lived in is not real at all, and that you can really choose the energy of goodness and calmness, it is there for you. Why did it take me 50 years to discover this truth? And now I see it, finally. I long for everyone else to see it for themselves. Then they, especially in the UK, would stop such endless harsh judgment.

From: Beatrice
To: Mummy
Hi Mummy,
I'm going to sleep right now. I wanted to say I love you so much and that I think of you every moment of every day. I carry you in my heart in everything I do. I am so proud of you and your amazing journey you are taking and thank you every moment that you are the role model you are and for being true to yourself. I love you so so much.

Beatrice

DIARY ENTRY

July 30, 2010

I am feeling like a lion cub that has just been sent out into the African bush to grow into a big lion. To fend for itself. It feels really extraordinary. I just want to stop on the side of a road, or a hillside, or in a garden, and just stop. I want to just make time to stand and stare. I have big eyes at the world, at what it all is and how fast it all goes.

I am very determined and committed to heal and be a force of light. I will do anything to heal.

From: Jeannemarie

To: Sarah

Dearest Sarah,

Second-guessing takes up too much time and leads to mental mutilation. God loves you. There is only one of you. I value you as God does. Not everyone has to love us, and it's their choice and we have to be happy with that.

With all my love this evening,

Jeanne

11 | *The People-Pleaser*

I've finally accepted that it's fine if 50 percent of people don't like me. Hopefully, the other 50 percent do!

$\mathcal{A}$NOTHER BREAKTHROUGH CAME after Dr. Phil and I moved away from my troubled childhood and broached the treacherous territory of the scandal.

"Here is an important question," Dr. Phil began. "Why did you have such a need for approval that you had to come up with money for your friend, up to the point that you would put yourself in jeopardy and deny your own gut-level instinct?"

I responded that I felt my need for approval would fill up some hole in me, deliver some vital gift that I couldn't give myself. I have done this my entire life, trying out fresh strategies, hoping that people, anybody, would find me worthy. You'd think that by now, at age fifty-one, I'd be less worried about what people think, but I'm not.

Dr. Phil's eyes focused on mine, and he held on to the stare while he said without hesitation, "You behave like an addict. Approval for you is like alcohol to an alcoholic or a drug to a drug addict. Approval is your fix. You're addicted to approval and acceptance and you will do anything to get it."

I don't know how often it happens like this, when a single, unforeseen moment delivers a sizable chunk of what you've ever really needed in your life, but that's what happened at that moment, when Dr. Phil confronted me with this truth. He nailed it. I was so starved for approval. My feelings of self-worth came from others liking me and approving of me. My happiness was dependent on getting love and attention from others. Disapproval or rejection from others meant I wasn't good enough. My best feelings came from outside myself—from how other people or a particular person treated me. I couldn't handle pain, especially the pain of disapproval, rejection, abandonment, being shut out, isolated, or lonely. In short, people could throw me a few crumbs and I acted like it was a whole loaf.

If you've ever found yourself sacrificing your own principles to please someone else, you may be an approval addict like me. If you do this for too long, you won't even know who you are—or what you think—without having it filtered through someone else.

I don't want to turn this chapter into one of those heartless self-help stories, but, honestly, appreciate who you are. It kills me to think that I have been living so much of my life to make other people happy.

People-pleasing really springs from a lack of self-trust. If you feel fundamentally unworthy and have to constantly prove yourself, if you don't feel it's acceptable to set boundaries on your time and energy, if you believe you can't survive the disapproval of others, then you will give yourself away over and over again.

Instead of learning to take responsibility for your own happiness by loving and approving of yourself, you have handed yourself over to others for love and approval, making them responsible for your feelings.

This inner self-abandonment will always cause the deep pain of low self-esteem, making you dependent on others to validate your own sense of worth. The sad thing is that love is the most abundant thing in the universe. It is always within us and around us—if we can recognize it.

Living as an approval addict is a very hard way to live. You have to constantly make sure you look right, say the right thing, and do the right thing to get the needed love and approval. But then if it only takes one glance of disapproval or one unappreciative word to ruin our sense of self-worth, we're in bondage.

We don't have to be approved of by other people in order to feel good about ourselves. If all of us accepted who we truly are, we would come to find that "fitting in" and acceptance from others wouldn't even be an issue. Dr. Phil told me that I wouldn't crave approval so much if I gave it to myself. I knew I had a lot of work to do there. But I was determined.

"You've got to stay on guard," Dr. Phil advised. "Make sure this [referring to scandal] won't ever happen to you again."

I nodded. "I can't mess up," I said grimly. "I can't."

NUGGETS:

- Do not fear rejection. If you fear rejection, be aware that you're likely to feel better about yourself if you take the risk—even if it doesn't pay off this time. There is a famous quote, "To risk nothing is nothing." Therefore, I think we must seize life, and grow with it as a plant grows toward the light.
- Watch "FOMO"—Fear Of Missing Out. This will make you go down wrong paths.
- Do not kid yourself or talk yourself out of it, which is what I did with the Fake Sheikh. The most important person whom you need to be honest with is yourself. Once you lie to yourself, dishonesty will become the norm in all the other dimensions of your life. Every situation presents us with a choice: When we make negative judgments about ourselves and others we send out negative energy and the situation will explode. When we see the positivity in situations, then we send out positive energy that will make us bloom.
- Respond, rather than react. I am now more in the habit of saying, "I'll get back to you." That way, I can consider in the privacy of my own mind whether a request is something I want to do, and why.
- Before offering a favor to please someone else, ask yourself

106

whether your behavior will actually please the other person or if you are just assuming that it will.

DIARY ENTRY

August 14, 2010

I am beginning to really stop and think and listen to myself. I have come to realize that I have not been living, I have been existing. I have not relished the moments. I have not had time to stand and stare.

I look at myself, really, for the first time in 25 years and say: What is it I want? What is it that fills my day?

I am 50 now, and soon to be 51. I have been going at such a mind-blowing speed. But where have I been heading?

Beatrice and Eugenie both said they are grateful for the Fake Sheikh's entrapment, as it has saved their Mummy. They may just have an enormous point.

I have been complacent to the nth degree, running toward a destination that did not come, that seemed to be around the next corner, the next weekend, the next Monday.

Anyway, Yeats sums it up in this poem:

> *When you are old and grey and full of sleep,*
> *And nodding by the fire, take down this book,*
> *And slowly read, and dream of the soft look*
> *Your eyes had once, and of their shadows deep;*
>
> *How many loved your moments of glad grace,*
> *And loved your beauty with love false or true,*

But one man loved the pilgrim soul in you,
And loved the sorrows of your changing face;

And bending down beside the glowing bars,
Murmur, a little sadly, how Love fled
And paced upon the mountains overhead
And hid his face amid a crowd of stars.

Let me not wait until I am too old to enjoy myself and
thereby my world and thereby my God.

12 | *The Two Wolves*

When I get my life back, I will not let go of it.

I SPENT MANY HOURS digesting Dr. Phil's wisdom and reading and rereading my notes. I shared my progress and learnings with Anamika, who told me this Cherokee legend, the story of the two wolves:

A Cherokee elder was teaching his grandchildren about life. He said to them, "A fight is going on inside me. It is a terrible fight between two wolves. One wolf represents fear, anger, envy, sorrow, regret, greed, arrogance, hatefulness, and lies. The other stands for joy, peace, love, hope, humbleness, kindness, friendship, generosity, faith, and truth. This same fight is going on inside of you, and inside every other person, too."

The children thought about it for a minute. Then one child asked his grandfather, "Which wolf will win?"

The Cherokee elder replied, "The one you feed."

This ancient wisdom spoke loudly to me since I must admit that on my journey, I had been feeding almost equal parts of each wolf—and sometimes I even let them feed each other!

On my bad days, I'd feel very lost, with zero belief in myself. I sometimes shocked myself with what entered my mind: "You're not going to make it." "You're fat." "You're not good enough." This wolf looms large and scary at times. Sometimes I believed it would actually eat me up.

I realize, though, that the wolves are my own creation. I can just as easily feed the wolf that is filled with compassion, humility, love, grace, good humor, and action. It really is a matter of choice, even though when the wolves come, we don't think it is. We actually believe that that big bad wolf is going to eat us and forget that all we have to do is stop feeding it!

To do that, we have the most powerful weapon in our arsenal and that is our thoughts. Some people see roses and are sad because they have thorns—yet others rejoice that thorns have roses. We need to see, look, and believe differently if we wish to change our feelings and perceptions.

Beyond the notions of positive thinking, it's about shifting our attention and intention to what we WANT, from what we don't want. In my relationships, rather than spending time thinking about all the things people do that irritate me (and believe me, the list is long and I spend far too much time feeding that wolf), I get power, compassion, and energy when I focus on all the wonderful things people do that delight me (and that list is just as big, if not bigger).

My day is brighter, my energy higher, my joy wider when I give myself grace, remember my sense of humor, and do the things I need to do with integrity. It's a wonder why most of us end up feeding the nasty wolf because the joyful wolf is so much easier to be around.

NUGGETS:

- Think about how your day is going right now. Which wolf are you feeding?
- You can choose the nasty wolf, or that other wolf, the one that speaks of benevolent thoughts, acceptance, positive thinking, dedication, and self-love. It is totally down to you; you can choose the kind of day that you want.
- Be grateful for the positive and dwell on those times and situations that have brought you joy.
- See things differently; shine a light on those dark places in order for them to go away.
- Accept what life brings us in all its glory and all its emotion. Life is filled with tragedy and celebration, fullness and emptiness, sadness and joy; moving within these extremes is part of what it means to be human—to be alive.
- Energy goes where the focus goes—you have to choose the kind of day you want.

From: Simon

To: Sarah

Live every second and do not waste a single moment. You have good friends . . . be with them. You have wonderful daughters and a stalwart ex-husband who has been fantastically loyal. Just keep your head up and sit in the sun, read some good poetry, and reflect on the good things and the good people who are your friends.

Simon

13 | *I Swallowed a Duvet*

I couldn't even begin to tell you the fears and anxieties I've had. The only way I could cover it up was to laugh or eat.

$\mathcal{W}$HILE ON MY journey, I did not want to get chubby. Or should I say chubbier? I realized that my weight had been creeping up, and it would have been easy to pack on more pounds, since my antidote for the glums has always been to stick my nose in a food bag and eat and eat more food.

We have not talked yet about my body in this book. My body is a good womanly figure. I have a nice "up top" and enough down bottom to look shapely. I can hide a spare five or ten pounds if I dress carefully and wear mostly black.

I think that fifty-one is a good age, and I feel really good now, although the weight just doesn't fall off like it used to. I know I just have to work even harder.

As I write this book and relive the last twelve months through my diary entries, I realize with excitement I have come a long way.

Even so, I am painfully self-conscious about my body. Last year, I attended the wedding of Antony Clavel and Maria Novella in Capri, Italy. Both are special friends of Beatrice and Eugenie, and although a difference in age, my magical soul friends, too, and they gave me a bracelet of the Blessed Lady, which I treasure every day.

The night before the wedding, there was a formal party. I wriggled into my body-squishing Spanx so that my gown would fit. I walked into the party and all I could see were hundreds of Bond girl look-alikes. I'm sure none of them were wearing Spanx. This was all too much for me; I immediately felt like I had swallowed a duvet.

A fine and stunning girl called Katie, with a near perfect porcelain skin, came up and we chatted. I asked her about my endless problems with swollen ankles and hands, puffing up at certain times of the day. She felt my wrist and pushed my heart chakra. She said that my pulse was that of someone who had had a severe trauma, a death or a car crash.

"Have you had any of those?" Katie asked. She had no idea of what I had put myself through, since she doesn't watch television or read newspapers.

"Yes, I have been through such a punishing trauma that I do not know what to do." I was amazed by how well she picked up on my troubled nature.

"Maybe you should not strive so much for perfection; the fact that you are alive is a miracle."

Katie was so right. I left the crowd and sat alone for awhile in the ladies' loo until I could muster up enough courage to return to the party.

My weight issues probably started as a child. This is not just a perception. I look at my baby pictures, and there are my chipmunk cheeks popping out under my curly red hair. Meanwhile, there is my beautiful slim mother, not an ounce of fat on her figure. She was trim and fit—so were my father and sister—so this is how I thought I should be.

After my mother moved to Argentina, I tried to eat my pain away. I became a compulsive eater because of the comfort I needed. I still see symptoms of it today. Whenever I have a hole in my heart, I want to eat. And I think: That's how I must have felt when I was twelve. I was desperately in need of love from a woman. When there's nothing inside, I feel empty, and I need filling up. So I'd fill up with food, thinking that would solve it. I became a fat girl struggling to be in a slim body, engaged in a constant war with my weight.

By the time I was nineteen, dieting became an obsession. I knew the catechism of every diet out there. I knew low-fat. I knew low-carb. I knew high-protein. I knew all the different kinds of crash diets, including one I made up myself: living on black coffee and irregular, imbalanced meals. The end result was a jittery wreck, completely wired up, a woman who would faint in the middle of the afternoon.

During my palace days, I missed Andrew so much. Did food take the place of affection for me? Perhaps. One thing I know: Overeating kept me from feeling things I didn't want to feel. If I started feeling anxious, or angry, or trapped, I practically ran to the kitchen. No one can deny that food is a great tranquilizer.

And on the cycle went; I didn't know how to break it. I'd have different sizes in my closet: 16, 14, and 12, and I'd have to mix and match them until something fit.

Later on, serving as spokesperson for Weight Watchers would literally save me. I was so lucky to work for a company that listened to the voice of real people with real lives, and gave real results. I was part of a giant embrace of goodness. I loved my time at Weight Watchers, and to this day I praise the friends I made. The leaders, who helped so many people to change their lives, lived and breathed the lifestyle plan, and I do too. Weight Watchers is always there for you, always at the end of the street. Linda Carelli and Sharon Riguzzi both changed my life, and I shall never forget the wisdom I learned in the twelve years I was the spokesperson. Linda and Sharon have passed away now, and I know if they were alive, I would have spent many a moment with them, seeking advice and wise counsel.

In the past, the British press had been so vicious, unrelenting, really, in making mockery of my weight. I can remember everything bad about my weight that has been said or written. I was forever compared to my best friend and sister-in-law, Princess Diana, who, of course, was quite slim. By contrast, I was called the Princess of Pork or Frumpy Fergie. If one newspaper reporter called me fat and ten others thought me pretty, I would believe the worst every time and carry it with me the rest of the day.

But the article that took first prize was a story claiming 82 percent would rather sleep with a goat than Fergie! (I'm afraid that I was far enough gone not to question the judgment of the other 18 percent.) Featured in one of the heavier-breathing tabloids, it was for me unforgettable.

Many other snipes have been made about my weight. Obviously, I could go on. From talking to other women, I know we all have a list like mine in our heads. We just don't forget.

These statements make me feel horrible to this day. Being fat, even a little bit fat, gets me very depressed. Sometimes, I hardly remember places or situations, just how my body looked in the mirror at the time. Whenever I think of all the things everyone says about me, my insatiable desire for comfort food kicks in, and I lose control of my food pattern. Once that happens I beat myself up even more because I've lost control of my eating.

DIARY ENTRY

I long to jump with excitement when all the boys say, "Let's go swimming in the sea, right now, and be back in time for drinks at sunset." I long to throw on a pair of blue jeans and not have to find a shirt that is long enough to cover the backside!

No chance in hell will I ever be able to slink into anything like a bikini. I didn't even want to wear my black swimsuit or my black sarong in which I could hide my fatness. I left both in London.

This self-torment all has to stop. I have to get fit, brown, and thin. I have to, and it all comes down to mind-set, determination, surrender. I have a long, long journey ahead. After sitting for one and a half hours in torrential rain and diabolical traffic, I sobbed into a 6:30 PM meeting, with not a stitch of makeup on and feeling like a frump. I looked like a fat, ugly, rain-sodden person, and my hair is cut shorter so I look older, like an old woman who no longer cares. I have to get in shape, into fitness, into discipline, and tell the dark torment to shut up.

Who needs the media to tell me I'm fat and frumpy? Obviously, I don't need help; I can do it all by myself.

I think it's important for you to know that I'm human like that. I honestly know deep down that I am a very good person. But I slide back when I hear people saying: "You're bad" or "You're fat."

I do have to spend my whole life worrying about my weight. My naughty comfort-eating moments that tempt me, when I am trying to fill the void, the no-man's-land in my heart, is mayonnaise, French bread with salted butter, Cheddar cheese and tomatoes, sausage rolls, and my egg salad sandwiches! I enjoy diet colas and have an affinity toward M&M's and savory foods. In fact, I love prosciutto ham so much that an Italian boyfriend once said that all the pigs tremble when I arrive in Italy.

Logically, I know that when you are as thin as you can ever imagine, the people who didn't love you before will still not love you, and the people who did love you before will love you still. People will come, go, leave, and die, no matter how much you weigh. I try to remember this, even though I constantly struggle with my weight.

While working on the docuseries, I was determined to get fit, inside and out. I did not want to turn into a big fat mess. I would abide by the Latin mantra "Mens sana in corpore sano." Translated, this means "a healthy mind resides in a healthy body." To do this I would address my body, with all the intensity of a golfer addressing a ball.

A chef called Angella Cole is a handsome, lovely lady I met when I was filming the docuseries in Malibu. She came every day with her magic wand in the shape of a wooden spoon! Angella has a store called Picky Eaters in Los Angeles, and she gave me all her delicacies. I was able to enjoy and eat them. They were gluten free, with lots of goodness, full of vegetables and protein, too.

I am still constantly looking for ways to enjoy my favorite foods while counting all the fat, calories, and carbs that have become my nemeses. So when I find a healthier alternative to a food I used to be able to enjoy without consequence, it's nearly akin to winning the lottery.

My latest jackpot was lamb lasagna. When I was a little girl, we'd often have roast lamb for supper. Afterward, the leftovers would be put into a mincer, pushed down with a wooden instrument, and ground finely enough to cook into a shepherd's pie. Angela made lasagna that way, with eggplant and tomato sauce, but no cheese. She came through, and her lasagna was to die for.

The best cleanse for the kidneys and for detox is what I call "green sludge." I have been drinking this for many years. I asked Angella to try the recipe. Adding her brilliance, she proceeded to toss bits of fresh apple, celery, asparagus, and other veggies into a blender and liquefied them.

Mostly I ate a fiercely healthy diet in California, and often dined on vegetables and fruits. I began to find ultimate joy in slicing a big, juicy tomato and eating it with just the right amount of salt.

I'm sure you're thinking, "Poor girl, I guess this is what the contemplative life has done to her."

My little happy friend who trains me, Sherri Cobb, jumped on a flight to Montecito, all at her own expense, to stand loyally by my side. She is based in New York and a talented artist. My Sherri Berri, as I call her, has the most golden heart, and I am so fond of her. What loyalty to drop everything to help me!

Sherri knew that the psychological trauma of the scandal had apparently manifested itself in my body. Sherri kindly told me that my muscles had certainly seen better days; they were as stiff as old bleach bottles. She suggested something called Muscle Activation Therapy, or MAT. It pinpoints which muscles are underperforming or not performing and stimulates them back into action. Through MAT, I'd stay agile enough and get better results from exercising.

She put me in a position and applied resistance against a particular muscle to see if it was active or inactive. She asked me to concentrate on my body, to experience it, something I usually try to avoid. If a muscle was jerky against the resistance, that meant it wasn't working properly. She'd then massage it to get the blessed thing pliable enough and less jerky. It was strange how I could feel a difference before and after. Inactive muscles came awake all over my body, most of them complaining and trying to go back to sleep.

I now actually like exercising better than ever. My body moves more fluidly, and doesn't creak as much. I'm moderate about exercise though. I don't believe we should all look like gladiators. We are meant to be active and strong so that we can perform tasks in our lives. That means walking without having to bring an oxygen mask, and maintaining a reasonably strong body. I've promised myself I'll stay on the path of moderation.

And I've done so. As I wrote in my diary one day: *I rushed to the paddle courts today, in desperate need of a lesson from Manolo, the paddle coach. He kept telling me that the whole point of the paddle is to be consistent, not to lose but be beaten, relax, and use your mind—and do this in your regular life, not just on the paddle court.*

I'd love to weigh 140 again like I did during my Weight Watchers days. But I'm not going to do it by subsisting on three lettuce leaves a day and swimming to France and back.

One important element in my health regimen is taking five omega-3 capsules a day. We don't eat enough fish in our diet, so I believe this is the key to my health and well-being. My hair and nails are growing strong, my cholesterol levels are good, and I feel strongly that omega-3 fatty acids are the key to keeping my veins and heart healthy.

In fact, I believe in it with such strength that I traveled to the north of Norway. I went to the Cod Liver Museum, and studied the benefits of omega-3 fatty acids. The brand I take is GO³, as it is so pure and comes from the north of Norway. I asked a spry, elderly gentleman who works at the museum why he looked so good. He had no wrinkles, not even on his hands. He attributed all to cod liver oil, which he had taken all his life. As a fisherman he handled cod liver all his life.

In World War II, the Germans wanted to give omega-3 to their troops to keep them healthy. As they reached northern Norway, the British and Norwegians fought not to let them have such a valuable weapon, and burned the cod liver oil factories down to prevent the Germans from getting the cod liver oil. It is soothing gold dust for the body. I feel so much better taking it, and my skin feels naturally moisturized.

I also drink grated ginger root with hot water; this is the oldest form of disinfectant for the body. I love watercress and have many cups of watercress soup during the day. I believe it gives me all the iron I need.

For many years, I have been the ambassador of the heart for Dr. Valentin Fuster at Mount Sinai Hospital. He is the legend of the heart. There is NO greater heart guru than Valentin Fuster, and he is my friend. We have many discussions on the heart, and I love to sit and listen to his soothing Spanish voice telling me all of the latest information in heart health. He is my hero, and that is why I say I am his ambassador!

I have to say that I love feeling healthy. Kate Moss was so right when she said that nothing tastes as good as feeling thin! I am not there yet, but I know my heart is in the right place.

NUGGETS:

- Free the mind and the weight will follow. By that I mean look after yourself. Drink plenty of water. Go for a run. Detox your body. Eat plenty of fiber. See sugar as an enemy. If you follow these simple suggestions, you will lose weight.
- Find someone who'll support you and provide motivation. My trainer keeps me committed by providing encouragement and guidance. I always call my trainer a buddy. If you haven't got a trainer, get out there and do it yourself—which is what I do now. I also find it very important never to go grocery shopping when hungry.
- Tell people you want to lose weight so that they don't bring you tempting treats. Unless you do this, they become enablers, and you'll feel guilty if you don't eat what they give you.
- If you're a comfort eater like me, work on breaking the habit. Do a self-exploration to find out what's triggering it psycholog-

ically. Keep a diary that includes information about how you were feeling and who you were interacting with right before a craving hit. Once you identify why and at what point you become out of control, mentally rehearse how you can handle this next time. Think of alternative ways to break your habit, such as walking out of the kitchen or having a glass of water.

- I've had to work hard on not comparing my body to other women's. Everyone is different. We all come in an array of pleasing sizes and shapes. Our job is to make the best of ours.
- The next time you catch a glimpse of yourself in the mirror, at least acknowledge yourself and don't look away.

From: Sarah S.

To: Sarah

Don't give your critics oxygen. I know what happens with you when you are alone. You allow The Fear to come and occupy your brain. Your mind goes into overdrive and allows negativity to creep in. When you are busy and engaged with people and friends, you allow yourself to put the past behind you. You can't rewrite the past and you have to stop torturing yourself. Those of us who know and love you know the happiness and fun and good you have brought to our lives. As I've said before: To know you is to adore you ... I know I do.

Love you and miss you madly

Sarah

14 | *The Miracle Man*

The lighter you travel, the farther and higher you can go.

*A*FTER MY SESSIONS with Dr. Phil, I met with Mark Nepo at his home in Kalamazoo, Michigan. An acclaimed poet and philosopher, Mark is the author of the brilliant books *The Book of Awakening, Facing the Lion,* and others. I found him to be a giant of humility, with profound kindness and wisdom, and one of the most spiritual beings I have ever met. I felt uplifted simply to meet him. We bonded through the amusing discovery that both of us trip over our own garbage.

The purpose of our meeting was to share notes on what it means to be alive.

This is a question that has puzzled saints and sinners and poets and philosophers since the beginning of mankind. It is a question that sooner or later is asked by each of us in our own lives. As I have grown a lot older and hopefully a tiny bit wiser, I have come to realize that this question has billions of answers on earth right now, because each of us has to find the meaning in our own life.

Mark Nepo knows more about this question than most. You see, in 1986, Mark, apparently healthy and age forty-two at the time, was diagnosed with a rare form of cancer.

I asked him to share his story.

Mark had been in Rome, studying Michelangelo's ceiling in the Sistine Chapel. He noticed a slight lump on his head. But he didn't dwell on the bump, so fired was his imagination by Michelangelo's artistry. But the bump continued to grow after he got home.

Mark had a CAT scan and an MRI taken of his head. They revealed a large tumor that was pressing on his brain. The skull had deteriorated in that area. Mark's doctor referred him to a neurosurgeon.

"The tumor was on the right, the creative side of my brain. That didn't help with my fears."

He was scheduled for a craniotomy.

"I was all hooked up with IVs and was getting the antiseizure drug Dilantin in preparation for surgery," he said. "They had shaved and shampooed my head."

But the neurosurgeon didn't feel right about going through with the operation. He wanted Mark to see one more specialist and take more tests. The results: lymph node cancer. So instead of having brain surgery, Mark was referred to an oncologist.

"I just plummeted. I was thrown into a state of constant uncertainty."

Treatment was prescribed: five weeks of daily whole-head radiation to be followed by an aggressive program of chemotherapy.

"They told me the radiation could affect my higher cognitive function," Mark said. "I'm a poet. That's where I live. I was terrified. It could affect my memory, my writing, all my gifts."

Mark's unusual tumor was reviewed by a board of specialists at the hospital.

Then, a miracle.

"At 8:00 AM, I was scheduled to have the spot on my head tattooed where they were going to shoot in the radiation. The board called at 7:00 AM and said to hold off because their review was inconclusive."

Just as quickly and as inexplicably as the fist-size tumor had mushroomed on the right side of Mark's head, it had vanished without a trace, and, more incredibly, without any treatment.

Surgery was called off for good.

"In the end, what I have now is the delight, the awe, that for some reason I received a miracle and my tumor disappeared. That's changed the way I perceive everything," he said.

Mark is Jewish, yet during his illness a Catholic priest prayed and laid hands over him, and he welcomed it. People brought religious icons to his house. He had Sufi friends who were praying for him. Other friends who were into holistic medicine sent him vitamins. He did intense visualizations. He tried everything and turned down nothing. Somehow it all added up to making him more available to God.

"The lesson of the miracle was that all of the things we have in common, and not the things that separate us, are what is important.

We have to be open to all forms of God. I can't close myself off as a Jew because a priest calls on Jesus to help me. The miracle came from a place where all these endeavors meet and I was fortunate to be so desperate that I went there."

In the hours I was privileged to spend with this inspirational man, we talked of many things: God, healing, faith, and transformation.

Toward the end, without my realizing it, he turned the conversation back to me. With his eyes trained on me, he asked, "Why do you let obstacles stand in your way? Whether we like it or not, obstacles in life are here to teach us."

Mark explained to me that our ability to live fully depends greatly on how we resolve and integrate our struggles. We talked about how a beautiful example for us exists in the metamorphosis from a caterpillar to a butterfly. Caterpillars don't just wall up and sprout wings. Within the chrysalis they literally dissolve into a formless, undifferentiated puddle of goo. Then the cells of this puddle mysteriously reorganize themselves into a completely different creature, a creature capable of realizing hopes the caterpillar never imagined, a creature that knows how to fly. When this creature—the butterfly—is ready to break free, a tiny opening forms, and the butterfly must struggle to get through it. This is life's way of forcing fluid from the body of the butterfly onto its wings so that it will be ready for flight once it achieves freedom from the cocoon.

He was right, of course. Sometimes struggles are exactly what we need in our lives. Challenges, restraints, setbacks—these were all things to push against to grow stronger. The struggles are a part of our journey and are preparing us for what awaits.

There is no triumph without struggle, no wisdom without misjudgment, no character without getting knocked down and picking yourself up again.

If Mark could recover from his monstrous cancer, using the gift of a poet to turn into a healing force, how could I be consumed by my recent brush with infamy? It was time to stop castigating myself for every false step I took and connect with all the good inside.

I take Mark Nepo with me everywhere I go. Not literally, but figuratively, by way of his inspiring books. If you picked up my personal copies of his books, you'd find dog-eared pages, folded-down pages, and frenetic underlinings. I always find myself writing excited margin notes—"yes, yes, yes!!!"—throughout every chapter. For example: If you wall up yourself against the world, then you wall inside yourself, then the light cannot get in . . . The word "courage" means to stand by one's core, and then that means to heal . . . See the old habits as old habits and get a new habit to replace old habits . . . Befriend your own gifts . . . The word "vulnerable" means to carry a wound graciously . . . Sift through what is ringing true and separate what is not and don't separate from your true self.

Mark taught me that I had to grow as a person and stretch my soul in good times and bad, and that is precisely what makes the journey, no matter how hard, so important.

NUGGETS:

- No matter what you have to face in life, do it with courage and honesty. If you fall off your pony, dust yourself off and get back on. And it hurts.
- Adversity does not have to destroy you. Your faith is there for you to rely on. You are not alone, but we always think we are—stop reaching out and reach in.
- Miracles are not out of the question. No matter how many

doors have closed, no matter how much bitterness and anger you feel, find the spiritual strength to keep an open mind and an open heart. The universe keeps back what you put out. Put out love and harmony, and you will get the compassion and tolerance and happiness.

- KBO: Keep Battling On. The morning might be sunny, but soon the sun will set and rise again the following day. It always does; you can rely on that and your problems will too.
- Dirty dishes get dirtier and hard to clean when you leave them out overnight. Meet your problems head-on, don't leave them in the sink.

> From: Sarah S.
>
> To: Sarah
>
> Personally, I think you have been amazing. You have picked yourself up, faced the music, and have done all that basically alone. I couldn't do it. You have an extraordinary inner strength which you mustn't doubt and that does not mean you have to pretend to be strong when you feel vulnerable. At times of uncertainty, you must lean on your friends. That is what we are all here for. Try not to worry about what people you don't know think. The people who are lucky enough to know you LOVE you. They see beyond human mistakes. Don't judge yourself so harshly, and don't despair . . . suddenly life will look rosy again, and you'll be back on top.

DIARY ENTRY

August 17, 2010

What on earth can be better than Mark Nepo's words: "Then God enters us like a brilliant stone falling in a lake, and the past ripples behind us, and the future ripples before us, and we are breathing in eternity." Thank heavens for Mark and his ability to ground me every day.

Thank heavens I am breathing and that last night a huge rainstorm (the likes of which I have never seen) nurtured the parched trees and plants. It appears that the whole garden is singing in gratitude.

From: Angela

To: Sarah

My dearest Sarah,

You are remarkable . . . you are able to write as you live: straight from your heart . . . no stops along the way. You somehow breathe life into words, and as I read them, I can see your face, feel your surroundings, and get to experience the journey with you. What an incredible "sharing" and life lesson for your daughters. How wonderful for you! Enjoying the moments . . . living in the moment is what it's all about. This discovery, I'm sure, will bring with it new insights and new avenues to pursue that will make so much sense going forward. I am so proud of you.

Angela

DIARY ENTRIES

August 19, 2010

I had a day from hell. I was again betrayed to the newspapers by a former member of my staff who was close to me and the girls. She painted a picture of me to the Sun newspaper that

I was similar to Marie Antoinette, that I was completely out of control and almost demonic.

I was so broken that I took to my room, and felt sick. Sick to my roots. Was I such a dreadful, horrid person? I suppose I must be. Have I done so much damage to so many? Am I really this outrageous person?

Anamika called me out of the blue, just at the right time, to remind me that I am not on my own. God is within me, and I was wallowing in self-hatred, thereby not letting God in. Anamika then said the best advice is to go down to dinner with Beatrice and Eugenie and feel their love.

I did so, and immersed myself in their young friends and the goodness of great people. I spoke with one of their male friends, Jamie, for over an hour about God. He confided that he had never spoken so openly to anyone about how he felt about God. His reaction reassured me yet again of my own God within myself. Miracles do happen every day.

Yet for four hours I struggled and fought and questioned and tormented myself. Then I stood up. I immersed myself in Mark Nepo's book. His words told me to forgive my past madness and move forward, mini step by mini step. I realized that although we go through muddy waters, the sun will shine again on the stillness of clear, calm waters.

August 20, 2010
My heart has been touched so many times by so many today and in the last few days. I have been tearful many times, and I can only believe and pray that this is a good thing, as my

heart cracks open, and for the first time I lower the shield and allow love and compassion in.

I need to and must love myself. I have to be the mother to myself that I never had, and the mother I am to my own lovely daughters.

It hurts daily to allow the heart to open again, but through the love of my children and the love of people, I am now beginning to see and feel. I just might get well.

15 | "*I Am a Thousand Winds That Blow*"

Acknowledge the life around you, no matter how inconsequential, and mesh your tempo with the rhythms of nature.

I REFLECTED ON Mark Nepo's brush with death, and I thought about how, in the course of three years, our family endured three tragic deaths: Princess Diana; my beloved mother, Susan Barrantes (which I shared earlier); and Carolyn Cotterell, my best friend. Shortly thereafter my father was diagnosed with terminal prostate cancer and for the next six years we shared in his valiant fight, hoping to beat it.

Carolyn was only forty-three years old when she died, with three young children. She was my best friend, my guardian angel, among the greatest teachers in my life.

We went back nearly twenty years when we were young and single and striving to make our way in London. Carolyn rented me a room in her apartment for fifty dollars a week. All I owned was a narrow bed and a set of drawers, but I also had Carolyn, the perfect roommate. She took me under her wing when I was a mess of insecurities. She listened patiently to my weight problems and makeup problems and boyfriend problems, and gave her gentle counsel when asked.

Later on, after I'd worn out my welcome in Buckingham Palace, she would say to me, "Fergatross [her pet name for me], just remember this: You walked into the Royal Family in blue jeans, and you can walk out in blue jeans. You have yourself, and you don't need anything more."

I had relied on Carolyn my whole life yet she never seemed to find me a burden. She gladly became godmother to Beatrice, and I became godmother to her daughter, Poppy.

The end began with a freckle, a tiny mole on her foot. With violent speed, the mole became a melanoma running up her leg and beyond. There were crushing treatments and moments of hope, but the cancer would run its course.

I last saw Carolyn at her friends' home in Los Angeles between rounds of chemotherapy. I asked her how she was standing the pain. A strong and spiritual Catholic, Carolyn told me that when she lay awake at night, she would look at her little Blessed Lady, kept near her bed, "and it gives me the strength to know that I'm not on my own."

As I made to go, Carolyn said, "Please take my Blessed Lady with you."

"I can't do that," I said.

And Carolyn, with typical foresight, said, "You will need it more than I will."

When she died, not long thereafter, I could not see how I could live without her. I felt numb, inconsolable. For weeks I walked through the motions of living, unsure of its point.

One night, about to go to sleep, I glanced at the Blessed Lady, which I keep with me wherever I go. I felt suffused with a warm feeling of Carolyn, who gave to the end. She will live on inside me as long as I draw breath.

Diana's death left a God-size hole in my heart. I loved her so much. Diana was one of the quickest wits I knew; nobody made me laugh like she did. We were like siblings—actually, our mothers, who went to school together, were also best friends. We took vacations together with our children. I snapped the photo Diana once used for her Christmas card.

It is true that our friendship was periodically strained. Sadly, at the end we hadn't spoken for a year, though I never knew the reason, except that once Diana got something in her head, it stuck there for a while. I wrote letters, thinking whatever happened didn't matter, let's sort it out. And I knew she'd come back. In fact, the day before she died she rang a friend of mine and said, "Where's that Red? I want to talk to her."

In any sibling relationship, there are ups and downs and peaks and troughs, but we were always steadfast in our friendship. We never let the sun go down on too many heated discussions. Our bond was never broken.

The night of the tragic crash in Paris, I was in Italy. After I got the call that Dodi Fayed had been killed, I immediately dialed Diana's mobile phone and left a final, haunting voice mail, saying, "Duch [the princess's longtime nickname], I'm here. How can I get to you?" I then tried to hire a plane to take me to Paris to be with Diana, before learning it was too late.

She was just thirty-six. It seemed impossible. How could something like this happen? Her sudden death, like my mother's, just didn't make any sense to me. Diana was not finished with her work here on earth.

Her passing left me devastated, but it was no less terrible for Beatrice and Eugenie, who were just nine and seven years old when Diana died. I'd been raised in the ways of the British "stiff upper lip" that culturally compels us to hide our emotions and show reserve and strength in times of adversity. It never felt natural to me to stuff my feelings and it is something I've discouraged in my girls. In our family, any loss deep enough to grieve deserves our heartfelt emotions. With Diana's death, my own emotions jumped between shock and inconsolable sorrow. Beatrice and Eugenie cried initially and then went silent. For them, Diana's death was frightening because their cousins' mother was dead, and it scared them that one day I, too, might not come home. They loved Auntie Duch.

Diana's tragic death fundamentally changed the British people, who were unaccustomed to seeing such a widespread show of raw, heartfelt emotion. There were no stiff upper lips as men, women, and children wept openly and added to astonishing mounds of bouquets and cards left in Diana's honor. Everyone was moved by our prime minister's tearful tribute to the Princess of Wales, to whom he referred as "the people's princess."

Britons expect and appreciate the Royal Family's show of strength during difficult times, but in the days following Diana's death their normal stoicism was widely and, I think, unfairly criticized. Anticipating enormous crowds in London on the day of Diana's funeral, Buckingham Palace doubled the cortege route between Kensington Palace and Westminster Abbey. Another hundred thousand descended on Hyde Park to view the funeral service on giant projection screens, and thousands more lined the seventy-seven-mile stretch of highway to see Diana's hearse en route to her bucolic ancestral home, where she is buried.

After Diana's death, my challenge wasn't how to fill the void, but how to live with it, how to make that space that hurts so much find its proper place in my life. I still say good night to Diana and Carolyn. I miss them every minute of every day. They were my sisters.

My parents never spoke of death to my sister Jane and me, but you could still tell when someone had died because of my mum and dad's somber mood and hushed tone of voice. This made me think dying was unspeakably horrible, and it is little wonder that the sight of Mum and Dad in their black funeral clothes gave me nightmares.

This is not to say that I think death should be made pretty or easy. In fact, I believe in facing death and loss with total honesty, because unless we experience its pain, we will have difficulty moving forward.

Beatrice and Eugenie had experienced the sudden deaths of Diana and my mother, but it was my father's cancer that made them witness the kind of gradual death that comes with terminal illness. Dad was a big, colorful grandfather to my girls, loved for his wicked wit and owl-like eyebrows. They would brush them with their Barbie toy hair brushes. He'd been the picture of health until 1996 when, out of the blue, he called us.

"The doctor did some tests. I have cancer. Prostate cancer. But wait—I'm not finished yet. They caught it early enough. I'll have some radiotherapy, and I'll be just fine."

We were stunned. He'd had no symptoms at all.

After the shock of the diagnosis, our family descended into an icy fog of fear. But not my father. He was determined not to be beaten by it and the thought of death never entered his mind. He wouldn't let anything get him down.

Statistically, the report meant this: My father's rate of cure was optimistic. In any group of three patients, only one is likely to die from this type of cancer. My dad, typically, responded that he felt sorry for the unlucky bloke.

For the next three months Dad had daily doses of radiotherapy and went into remission for several years. Then, in 2001, the cancer returned.

Confused, maybe even panicked, we helped him focus on treatment decisions that would help try to save his life. He could not have radiotherapy twice, and he refused hormone treatment, which could cause impotence.

Dad continued playing cricket and lived as normal a life as possible. He needed my stepmother in ways he'd never needed her before, and she was there for him, every step of the way, with patience, encouragement, and deep abiding love.

It was, nonetheless, a stressful, trying time for everyone. I plastered a smile on my face and tried to maintain a positive outlook, but the fact is I was terrified. We all were.

Along the way, I formed some very definite opinions I knew I would want to share. If your husband is facing prostate cancer, listen to the doctor but do your homework. Find a support group, and become a one-woman support group for your husband. This disease goes to the very heart of his manhood.

In November 2003, Dad collapsed, having suffered a suspected heart attack, and was admitted to hospital. His last words to me were, "Well, you and your sister get your great legs from me, not your mother." He then said, "Remember the show has to go on."

Dad rallied after suffering a second heart attack but, at the end of a long struggle, his condition deteriorated and he passed away. Beatrice was twelve and Eugenie almost eleven. Dad had been in and out of the hospital for years, so there was no denying that one day he'd be gone.

When he died, I grieved, I cried. It seemed as though I'd be forever grieving. It was really tough. Emotions just went right through me. I kept going over it in my head and thinking of things

I should have said. I tried to move on; that's all I could do. Life got sadly different with Dad gone.

Strangely the slow progression of his illness allowed my girls to experience the preciousness of life and the meaning of peace and dignity in death. You see, when Dad was diagnosed, he did something extraordinarily brave. He took to the public stage as an advocate for prostate cancer prevention. Between stretches of therapy, my father gave countless media interviews and speeches all over Britain to illuminate the health issue most men try their hardest to ignore.

Offering words of hope to other cancer sufferers, he optimistically pronounced: "You can never get used to that word, cancer. Cancer is something that hits straightaway and because you hear about so many cases of people with cancer dying, immediately cancer is connected with death. But it doesn't have to be, far from it in my case. It doesn't have to be."

After Dad died, he was widely praised for his one-man campaign that surely saved many lives. For our family his legacy is one of courage, compassion, and selflessness.

Death struck Beatrice and Eugenie hard when their close friend James, just twenty-one, without warning or apparent reason, shot himself to death. James was the son of one of my best childhood friends and for the girls he was like their big brother. Beatrice, Eugenie, and I were inconsolable at James's funeral, heartbroken and mystified as to why someone so full of life and love decided to just end it all. We are determined to help Clare, James's mother, with the James Wentworth-Stanley Memorial Fund, which does research on teenage suicides, now the second-largest cause of death among young men age fifteen to forty-four in the UK. In 2006, there were 5,554 deaths, which amounts to about fifteen suicides a day, considerably more than traffic accidents.

When someone close dies everyone's world turns upside down. There is the initial shock followed by the whirlwind of contacting family and friends and preparing for the funeral. Then suddenly life is meant to get back to normal—as it should and must. Indeed, the healthiest thing a family can do is to pull together and share the stages of grief, coping, and healing.

When my friends and family must mourn the loss of a loved one, I send them this poem on grieving. It has helped me when those dear to my heart have moved on.

> *Do not stand at my grave and weep;*
> *I am not there. I do not sleep.*
> *I am a thousand winds that blow.*
> *I am the diamond glints on snow.*
> *I am the sunlight on ripened grain.*
> *I am the gentle autumn rain.*
> *When you awaken in the morning's hush,*
> *I am the swift uplifting rush*
> *Of quiet birds in circle flight.*
> *I am the soft stars that shine at night.*
> *Do not stand at my grave and cry;*
> *I am not there. I did not die.*

When I am at Royal Lodge, I rise early in the morning to walk through the woods. One day on my walk, my mind swirling with such anxiety, I stepped into a clearing, and a flock of birds clattered up from the trees. I gazed across the woodland, with its bluebells and wildflowers under the opening sky. It came to me that I want much more of this before I die. The irony followed: I often missed out on this blessing before because my mind would be troubled with something else. Now my walks are both a joy and a spiritual discipline. My task is simple, but difficult: Pay attention. See all of nature stirring before my every step. Hear the wind rustling through the tender leaves. Recognize how the world grows more and more beautiful every single day.

NUGGETS:

- Grief is a personal journey, and the time line of when you'll start to feel better is different for everyone. Know that you won't be in a place of grief forever, and as time passes, you'll hurt less often. If you look at your watch, it never stops for no man—it keeps on going and so will you.
- Be open to the lessons that can be learned from your painful experiences. If we are open to them, all the events in our lives—even painful ones—have the seed of something new and good. Advice is great but even with these nuggets do not rely on them—rely on yourself. Listen to everyone's advice, but make up your own mind.
- Do not hide, shirk, or flee from the pain. Allow yourself to experience it, but practice the virtue of endurance. Endure what cannot be changed. Live by the reality that you will grow stronger because of the experience.
- Let loved ones in. Allowing others to help you—whether by making phone calls or doing your grocery shopping—benefits you both: You'll have company in some of your burdens, and they'll feel good about lightening your load.

DIARY ENTRY

September 1, 2010

I spent time in New York City with Poppy, the daughter of my angelic friend Carolyn. Poppy is the photocopy of her mother. She is interning at the Gagosian Gallery, and shining tall and beautiful. One Thursday night, I invited Poppy over for a sleepover in my hotel room and gave her a pair of pajamas. When I shared a flat with her mother so many years ago, we gave each other rose-colored pajamas. I shared this story with Poppy as I handed the pajamas to her. It was a special moment between us. I hope she always feels my love, support, and comfort when she wears her rose pajamas. I offered Poppy a caveat though: Don't wear them when a good-looking boy is around!

16 | *No-Man's-Land*

Recognition, appreciation, and gratitude all grow in the heart when we have love, silence, compassion, and gentleness.

A FEW YEARS AGO, I woke up to an amusing headline (at least it wasn't destructive or libelous!). The British tabloids were reporting that I was about to become a Buddhist—simply because I met with the Dalai Lama on a recent visit to India.

Certainly, I am inclined toward spirituality. For me, faith and spirituality mean peace. At every stage of life, whether in hardship, loneliness, or bitterness, you feel peaceful inside, because you know that God is walking next to you, unseen, unheard but looking after you so that you will not fall down.

Becoming a mother has been a spiritually life-changing experience for me. It has made me grateful for being blessed with two gorgeous lives. Every time I see Beatrice and Eugenie I know without a doubt that there is a God. And that He resides in their sparkly lives. My girls are the best ambassadors of who I am. They're the one really good thing that I've done in my life and that can't be taken away from me. Eugenie has a fantastic creative flair. Beatrice is responsible and definitely born to be a princess. Both are respectful of life.

I know God must love me for giving me a considerate and compassionate man like Andrew and supportive and encouraging friends. I see God in everyone around me, and my idea of worship is to be loving and respectful for all that I come in contact with.

One very conscious effort I have made is to not start focusing on God only when there is something wrong in my life. I focus on Him when things are going well and thank Him every day for giving me a wonderful life. I have many spiritual guides, Buddha, Jesus, Babaji, Sai Baba, Mother Teresa, and many more who sacrificed their lives because they could see the God in them, and the God in them wanted them to sacrifice their lives for humanity so that we people could learn peace and purity. I am always open to learning and growing, spiritually.

Cultivating a spiritual connection can help you feel more grounded in life and broaden your perspective on the world. Study after study has found that spiritually active people experience greater happiness; this may be due to the close relationships that are engendered, to the sense of meaning and purpose people extract from their faith, and/or from the incentive people feel to extend the focus beyond themselves.

One of the most spiritual places on earth is India. I love the country and its people and culture for personal reasons. India has given me decades of discovery, learning, and friendships. India is in my heart.

When I met the Dalai Lama in the Indian border town of Dharamsala, where he has lived in exile for more than four decades, I asked him about how he dealt with regret. He said, "Regret is guilt. Guilt is a fabrication of your own mind. Learn from your past and go forward." His response felt like a fresh, clean page to me.

It wasn't until I got to fifty-one that I met with Rajesh Raman in Kamalaya, Thailand, and he started giving me daily spiritual sessions, which helped guide me to find myself. I believe Rajesh is a genius and an extremely personable mentor. And I am one of his people.

When you become aware of thoughts that are not real, then you get your life back. This is what I practice at home and this is what you can do.

It was many years ago that I was given a great gift by a lovely lady, a friend of mine. The gift was a man called Hugh Lillingston, who invented the Warrior Programme.

The Warrior Programme was established in 2007. It restores self-esteem, rebuilds confidence, and helps people to lead a more fulfilled life. The program addresses the complex challenges faced by those who are emotionally scarred by what they have been through.

Immediately, I went to see him on a one-on-one basis. Through this I have learned all about Neuro Linguistic Programming, which I have put into practice in my daily life. Apart from seeing him every day, I attended a four-day workshop in Ronda, Spain. The retreat program was about personal transformation. The most important skill for a human being is the ability to communicate. The practical understanding that your thoughts create your reality and therefore imagination is the key to put control in yourself. The four-day program led me to find out more about myself and to reach my goal of finding the true Sarah. I learned many new techniques to use in my life on a daily basis—some of these I will share with you.

The joy of what Hugh Lillingston does is he gives you hope. He makes you understand that we are not our thoughts.

Prioritize
Schedule
Communicate

Using the PSC goals has helped me put into action what I want to achieve in life and how I am going to do this. Questioning all the time what do I want, what makes me happy, and what values are important to me. Setting boundaries and deadlines that can be expanded as I grow and develop.

Using the techniques from the Warrior Programme helped me overcome negative feelings that we experience: What am I angry about? What am I sad about? What am I fearful of? What am I guilty about? By questioning ourselves and identifying the problems we can reach the goals we set before us in a controlled and positive way.

Probably the most valuable ideal I learned was how to stop negative thoughts controlling my everyday existence. Think that your mind is like a filing cabinet, divided into values and beliefs, attitudes, memories, language, decisions, time, and space. When we experience something negative, our minds then compare this to previous events, which is then how we feel about ourselves. If we become aware of this we can see it has created false thoughts.

A golden rule I wrote for myself is FEAR, which stands for:

F—False
E—Expectations
A—Appearing
R—Real

After this most important learning experience I felt I could stretch my arms out to help a very close friend. This is what I wrote,

> *You will wake up frightened as another day bids hello. Stop . . . whatever you are doing and go and sit quietly somewhere. Close your eyes and breathe. As you listen to your breath in and out, your mind and mind chatter will stop, as it has to focus on the in and out of breath. You are my friend, and I care deeply for you. You are so special. We have got to help you see your true self. So . . . whatever thoughts come in are not real, you have believed your own made-up thoughts, and they can ruin your day. You are doing well. You are a butterfly in a cocoon and you can fly. Your fears are filling you with anxiety. Fears of where, how, and when. In the silence and calmness you will see that. Imagine the thoughts as balloons full of mind . . . They come in, now see them as that and let them go. That is called awareness. And this is what true spirituality is. This is why the Dalai Lama monks prac-*

tice up to six hours a day to calm the mind and chatter. Just breathe. You are not on your own. I see your heart and soul and you are special and you are like so many people . . . It is frightening to realize that we have been asleep to ourselves for so long and now through awareness you are looking and waking up.

Now I am going to sit quietly for twenty minutes and listen to my breath and realize that my thoughts are not real and cannot thieve me of today. For the next weeks here I will be with you on text or in person and we will crack that heart open. I know it is frightening and you will want to fill that void . . . This is no-man's-land . . . But stay strong to trusting me and together you will see the answers . . . This is called spiritual work. And if I can do it . . . so can you.

NUGGETS:

- Stay where you are. Don't look up. Don't look left. Don't look right. Look down and sit in your space. You may be in a valley—a no-man's-land. It's frightening, but the valleys of life help us face our fears. Eventually we'll look up at the mountaintops. Life's mountaintops encourage us, but the work of healing is in the valleys. We live in the valley, the no-man's-land, but are sustained by the mountain.

- Replace "I can't" with "I can" and "I will." Yes, there may be temptation along the way to take the wrong path, but that doesn't mean we're failures; it means that we are progressing. If you feel like you're going in circles, that's good! Progress is never a straight path.

- When you come to a roadblock—or, better yet, before you encounter an impasse—read and learn from those who've gone before you.

- Your focus determines what you find in life. If you focus on opportunities, you'll find them. Focus on obstacles, and you'll find those.

From: Jane

To: Sarah

There are two beautiful sayings I heard today, one from John Daido Loori and one from a book called Perseverance *by Margaret J. Wheatley. I thought of you, my sissy poos!*

John Daido Loori (Zen teacher, 1931–2009): In reality, there's nothing anyone can give us. There's nothing that we lack. Each of us is perfect and complete, lacking nothing. This truth must be realized by each one of us. Great faith, great doubt, great determination are three essentials for that realization.

"The Path" by Margaret J. Wheatley

Great Doubt
Who am I?
Why am I here?
What's the point?
Why me?
How do I get out of this?

Great Faith
I am here for a reason.
I trust that I can learn and grow.

I trust that other people are worth the struggle.
I know that every situation is workable.

Great Determination
I am willing to keep going.
I choose to stay.
I surrender to what is.

From: Gloria
To: Sarah
Dear one,
Thinking of you at this moment and holding you close. Am so hoping life is on a more even keel and you are having a little break. I do so hope that one day our paths may cross so that we can have the big hug that we both need.

With love,
Gloria

From: Debbie
To: Sarah
Dear Sarah,
I just wanted you to know that I believe you will be able to rise like a "phoenix"—all the best people do.

Love,
Debbie

17 | *Healing in the Desert*

You can see magic anywhere if you look hard enough.

a PRECIOUS, SIGNIFICANT PART of my journey took place in Arizona—a state I love. Arizona has a magic all its own. Just being in its profound beauty opens up my soul, for this is a place that holds thousands of years of sacred history within its landscape of pastel-painted bluffs, buttes, otherworldly rock formations, and sunsets straight out of those old cowboy movies. It is here, where nature goes to such extremes, that so many people find emotional and spiritual awakening.

My first stop in Arizona was Cottonwood, one of those funky

155

places where you don't intend to stay, but that hooks you anyway. Although quirky and appealing, Cottonwood is an old farming town, and farming towns always have a rough look. It is surrounded by jagged mountains on the south, east, and west, and to the north by mesas and buttes. Named for the beautiful cottonwood trees that grow along the Verde River, Cottonwood has a population of around six thousand. The town sits roughly three-fourths of a mile in the air. There are shops and old houses strung on a couple of streets like beads on threads.

My docuseries crew and I were in town where I was to meet with a shaman named Clay Miller, and to be honest I felt a bit nervous about the whole thing. I didn't know what to expect. It was as if I had an appointment for which I was not ready.

Shamans have been around since the Stone Age. They are people of knowledge, visionaries revered as healers and holy persons in Native American, African, and other ancient cultures. Their beliefs do not constitute a single religion, although worldwide shamanic traditions approach reality and human experience in similar ways. In shamanic thinking, everyone and everything has a spirit, and spirits affect all events, including illness and disease. If you're depressed or ill, a shaman often will say that your condition was triggered by a traumatic event that broke off part of your soul, which is now trapped in the spirit world. He or she might perform a "soul retrieval," coaxing the lost piece home and "blowing" it back into your body.

An example might be that a husband took a piece of his wife's soul when he died because he could not bear to be apart from her. Once the husband is located, a shaman will communicate with him and ask him to relinquish the soul so his wife can live a full life again. The shaman will then travel back with the precious item, restore it to the wife, and help her feel whole again. The work of some shamans is said to be so powerful that they are believed to be capable of changing a person's life.

Clay's home was a small one-story brick structure, just off a dirt road. Wind chimes sung in the breeze, and various large dogs loped around the yard. I went inside and found Clay sitting cross-legged on a circular green woven rug in a sunlight-splashed room with his white husky, Honteyo, by his side. The walls of his home were decorated with bits of all types—skulls, feathers, rocks, birds, birds' nests, Native American artifacts, and various items that I deduced to be shamanic icons. There were many bookcases filled with books leaning this way and that. It all looked very spiritual, and you felt like you were inside a wigwam. A bottle of wine in the corner caught my eye, and I immediately thought, "Fine, at least he knows about Napa Valley, too."

Clay had thick shoulder-length salt-and-pepper braids. His eyes were hooded in a serene gaze. His sleeves were rolled up to show sinewy arms, and he wore dusty jeans. Tall and rugged, Clay impressed me as a dignified man, having something of an authoritative aura around him, with an unknown quality that must have been shamanic spirituality. I suppose he was my idea of what a shaman from Arizona ought to look like.

I sat down across from him. Honteyo was immediately drawn to me and plopped himself down in my lap. His white fur began to shed all over my black skirt and cardigan. Clay reassured me that Honteyo was simply checking me out. I scratched the back of the dog's ears.

"My dogs are not only my companions, they are my helpers," he explained. "Unless you have an aversion to dogs, they will accompany us on this shamanic journey. Their presence has been a

157

great blessing and gift to many. Some who have been afraid of dogs have overcome their fears and found new friends."

A dog lover myself, I was immediately struck by how much he loved his dogs. I was extremely curious about his work.

"People come to me for all sorts of things," Clay said. "I'm called out any time of the day or night, just like a doctor. Some people come to me with illness; others want me to intercede with the spirit world to end some misfortune. Everyone's shamanic journey is different. It can be about healing or it can be answers to questions of concern."

The shaman asked me what I was seeking. And I started telling him about how I'd been emotionally stuck over feelings of abandonment by my mother, about being beaten and persecuted by the scandal, and about feeling stratospherically sensitive to everything.

We went outside, and Clay directed me over to a pile of rocks and asked me to load them into a bag. I did as he asked, picking up the heaviest rocks in the pile, without a clue as to why.

Before long, we jumped in his dusty SUV with Honteyo and another one of his dogs, a German shepherd mix, and found ourselves barreling along dirt roads through a flat, arid terrain dotted with cacti, juniper shrubs, and scrub oak and into the red-rock wilderness beyond. The shaman sang at the top of his lungs—a love song to Arizona—while one of his dogs barked incessantly. All I could think was: "What am I doing here?"

About thirty minutes later we got out of the car and he asked me to lug the bag of rocks with me. I still had no idea where this was going. I decided to take from the experience what I needed, and logic be hanged.

I was wearing Chanel ballet pumps, the worst shoes imaginable for hiking rocky, dusty terrain. Little did I know I had to lug the wretched rocks through Arizona desert.

I wobbled behind Clay up a rocky winding trail, before arriving on a beautiful little mesa. I have to admit, it was a vibe-y place. The silence that descended on us was unforced and magical, especially with what the Indians call the "footsteps of the wind," the sound breezes make as they dance through the openings in the rock face.

I looked at those mountains across a sweep of red rock and thought, "What if I didn't have to go home? What if I just stayed?"

On the mesa the shaman asked me to empty my bag of rocks.

"Out you go, love," I said, as the rocks came tumbling out.

"These are your issues," said the shaman.

I then realized that we all have our own bag of rocks to carry around throughout life, baggage we carry wherever we go. Mine were the rage and anger of Sarah being abandoned as a young twelve-year-old, and later having to sacrifice my marriage. I had never let go of the emotions tied to those events.

Next, Clay asked me to do exactly as he did. The shaman outstretched his muscled arms upward and started chanting to the spirits. Suddenly he dropped to his knees, screamed "Mum!" and started sobbing. What on earth was going on?

At that moment, I recalled my confirmation at Sunningdale Church when I was a little girl. My relatives sat stiff and proud in the pew. The service was austerely sublime. The whole affair went off perfectly in fact, until I came back from the altar and broke into a huge, beaming smile: then an audible siege of giggles.

Mum was slightly mortified. "Can't you take anything seriously?"

Of course it was shyness that made me giggle back then, and it was shyness that was about to make me giggle now, looking at Clay on the desert floor, shouting "Mum." I was desperate for fellow gigglers, but to my amazement, the entire crew and team were taking it all seriously. Now I looked a proper chump!

So then Clay asked me to do it. He said that by shouting my mother's name repeatedly, pain would be released. At first I felt so embarrassed and inhibited because the film crew was taping it. But I'm a good sport, so I screamed out loud . . . "Mum, why?"

I felt something had changed inside me. It wasn't so much a presence as an absence. At that moment, all that pain, rage, and anger I had carried seemed to have vanished. It was a clearing of some blockages that had held me captive for so long—a powerful emotional release. Clay made me look at my fears in a way I'd never done before. Although I still had a long way to go, I felt that I had begun to transform emotions such as fear, grief, anger, and shame into sources of strength and compassion.

From a shaman's perspective, there is always a way to transform the negative thoughts and emotions that we encounter throughout the course of our lives. What he explained to me is that if we choose to perceive negativity, anger, and fear all around us, that will be our experience. But if we move to a place of love and appreciation of self and life, our perception changes, creating light and love all around us.

"It's like if you saw a little girl crying, you'd go over to her and you'd just hold her tight," he said.

"Yes."

"So just hold yourself."

What Clay wanted me to see was that due to unresolved heartaches from my past, I wasn't all that I could be. I needed to start caring for the little Sarah within me—loving and nurturing the little girl within. The shaman saw that I had walled her off.

He was right, of course. I grew up without adequate emotional nurturing, and this may have led me to put all my effort into nurturing others, in hopes that they would reciprocate and tend to my needs. But this way of being in the world keeps us stuck in loving others too much, while ignoring our own needs. We exhaust ourselves trying to take care of everyone else, yet fail miserably at our responsibility to properly care for ourselves. I had to find the courage to turn within and look at myself with an attitude of love and acceptance, treating my vulnerable inner self with kindness and love.

The shaman made me see that I had ignored little Sarah for years. Now I had to imagine that I was holding this little girl close to my heart and embracing her in love. Little Sarah needed to know she was loved, acknowledged, and accepted unconditionally by me. She needed to trust that I would protect her, by thinking clearly and lovingly, and by saying "no" to fearful, critical, and self-sabotaging thoughts. Once I faced, acknowledged, and loved little Sarah, then and only then could I begin the process of developing a loving relationship with myself.

It was time to love little Sarah with all my heart. As I wrote in my diary: *It appears that the great mother I am to my daughters should have included me, my little Sarah. It has taken me twenty-one years to realize that I must embrace myself, and be kind and gentle to me.*

This was all a real awakening.

Before we left the desert, the shaman played his flute and serenaded me on the mesa top. I could feel another eruption of giggles bubbling under my rib cage, but I managed to suppress them.

Yes, at times my shamanic journey was humorous. Yet it gradually led me to realize: When we open our heart and unshutter our soul, we find unimagined things are suddenly possible. Clay is an amazing individual, very caring and kind. I loved how he sang to me—without inhibition or self-judgment, and that alone was a living lesson from which we can all learn. Every good person you meet in your life has something for us, if we would only recognize it.

I believe there's a powerful shamanic experience waiting for everybody—somewhere. It's just a question of deciding to go look for it. And listening when you find it.

NUGGETS:

- Be willing to let go of your inhibitions and worries that people are judging you. Everyone has insecurities; we are all only human.
- Look for guides in life, people who lift our spiritual vibrations and help us to feel better. Really listen to what they offer and act on their input.
- Acknowledge yourself as someone who is open to personal growth, change, and transformation.
- Explore something new that feels positive and meaningful—a shamanic journey, for example, or a spiritual retreat.
- No matter how well or how poorly your parents did their jobs, once you grow beyond childhood and adolescence, the challenge of nurturing yourself is yours, and yours alone. Feel your worth and start doing things that express self-love. And put on your own oxygen mask before helping others. Ask yourself in

what ways you blame others for what happens to you. Take responsibility for you own actions. Don't seek an immediate result; seek patience.

DIARY ENTRY

September 10, 2010

I have been so busy . . . being my own assistant, being a mother, writing a book, filming a docuseries, and trying to breathe. At times, it can be overwhelming. Anyway, my eyes are looking over the sunny Camelback Mountain of Phoenix. I am so glad to be back. I came here in June, shortly after the trauma of the scandal. I felt at home, at peace.

My daughters have given me total support with the docuseries, something I wrestle with every day. Most people work on themselves in total isolation, but I am doing it in front of two camera operators, one director, and a room full of spectators taking notes. I will admit that each and every spectator is relating so totally to the points discussed. That being so, I have a sense that the producers and network are correct, that this show will help so many people find themselves. I pray they are right.

It is terrifying to do this work so publicly. I know that the tight, closed lips of many British people will completely castigate and finally obliterate me from the British Isles—and practically existence—for airing my laundry in public. I remember when my dad was dying of prostate cancer, and he went on the radio to urge men to get checked, many called him up and told him to stop talking about it. Aaagh, the Great British stiff upper lip.

As all my guides have told me: They already despise you. There is only one way to go, and that's up and true to yourself!

They cannot be wrong.

From: Suki

To: Sarah

You are not an animal to be caged in. You are a being full of life and much to give and need to be free to fly and spread happiness. You have been born for a higher purpose. Realize the divinity within and all will start to make sense.

Suki

18 | *Into the Maze*

I use no rules to navigate so I can enjoy the ride.

*T*HE DAY AFTER my experience with Clay, I met with Martha Beck, probably the best-known life coach in the country since she started writing a regular column in Oprah Winfrey's O magazine and from her appearances on the *Oprah Winfrey Show*. I first met Martha in Phoenix in June 2010. She opened my eyes to the work of the mind and was a great gift from Oprah. We became sisters immediately. It was Martha who supported my doing the docuseries. I wrote all my diary entries, from June to now, to Martha and Oprah. I was happy to be reunited with her.

You'd think I wouldn't have much in common with a diminutive, soft-spoken life coach. But from the very first time I met Martha, I wanted to hug her and tell her, "Yes! That's me!" in her wonderful, wisdom-filled columns. Martha makes you glad that life can be so lived, so loved, so known, so rich in observation and feeling. Her writings are so rich in wisdom and her life story is incredible.

As a life coach, Martha helps people whose lives have gone off course find their way back to authentic, rewarding lives. She believes that any deep crisis is an opportunity to make your life extraordinary in some way—which is why I wanted to spend as much time with her as I could.

Joining us was Koelle Simpson, a lovely raven-haired woman, and a student of world-renowned equine trainer and bestselling author Monty Roberts, known as the Horse Whisperer. Koelle is brilliantly intuitive and, as an Equus Coach, a horse whisperer in her own right.

Martha and Koelle introduced me to some unique ways to help people overcome fears and find their true selves. The first exercise we did was to create a "vision board." A vision board is basically a collection of pictures and words, glued together on a poster board or foam board, that organizes one's goals and dreams. Images are cut from magazines, then organized and sorted to fill the board. Most people choose to place the board in a spot where they will see it every day so it reminds them of what they are working toward.

Martha explained that vision boarding "puts clarity and focus on your goals and can serve as a powerful reminder of how you should be spending your time."

Vision boarding acts as a focusing tool for your mind. We all have dreams of what we desire, yet we rarely capture them on paper. But an amazing thing happens when you put those images on a vision board. Your subconscious mind begins working on that idea or goal, even with no conscious effort on your part.

I cut out lots of different things in magazines that represented what I wanted to manifest in my life: women in sleek blue jeans; thin, fit women; images of the sea; India; all my dreams. When I saw the new possibilities right there on my vision board, my whole outlook on life began to change. Everything and anything seemed possible.

Before you read any further, why not try creating your own vision board? Gather all of your supplies: photos, magazines, glue, scissors, catalogs, markers, poster board, or any other items you'd like to use.

Cut out pictures from magazines that represent your dreams and desires. Choose pictures, items, and phrases to create a collage that represents what you want in your life.

Glue your images to a poster board. You can organize by theme — health, travel, relationships, wealth — or make it a random collage. Think of how you want your life to look in a year. Keep your vision board where you can see it for daily inspiration.

Mine was jam-packed with images to manifest my destiny and turn my desires into reality. This was a very powerful tool.

One day Martha announced that she was going to teach me how to weaken the power of my negativity.

As she spoke, I immediately took out my notebook, so I could jot down everything she said.

"Like many people with self-esteem problems, you probably think you're worthless, correct?"

I hesitated. "Yes, I tell myself that all the time. I think there is something inherently wrong with me, something that leads people to find me unappealing. And I don't ever want to do anything that could result in criticism from other people."

Martha asked me if I was willing to do a little experiment—something that's used to challenge negative thoughts and unhealthy beliefs.

"Of course," I said.

"How does this belief that 'you're worthless' make you feel?"

I pondered the question for a moment. "Depressed, helpless, unlovable."

"Exactly. Negative thoughts can drag you down into a spiral of anxiety or depression."

Martha went on. "It's good to be aware of how your thoughts and beliefs make you feel. That's the first step toward changing them. Next, let's challenge that belief in a rational way. Okay, you think you're worthless. What proof do you have that this is true?"

"I made a horrible mistake. That proves I'm imperfect and therefore I'm worthless."

"Not exactly. That you are imperfect is shown by your mistake—we all make mistakes—but it doesn't logically follow that you are worthless, does it?"

I agreed that my conclusions were completely illogical.

Martha continued. "Your belief of being worthless—can you describe any experiences that prove this belief is untrue?"

"Well, my children love me. Many people support me. I have accomplished much good in my life. I have a brilliant mind."

"So how does it follow that you're worthless?" Martha countered.

I pondered that for a moment. "I'm not sure I ever thought about it like that. I guess I'm not worthless."

Martha suggested, too, that I test out newer, healthier beliefs to see whether they made more sense. So instead of saying to myself, "I'm worthless," I should look for more evidence that I'm a worthwhile person.

The aim of this exercise is simply to help us really look at our unhealthy beliefs, scrutinize them by checking any evidence that is contrary to such beliefs, and begin to discover more logical, healthy perspectives. Anyone can do this; it's a way to get the answers we're looking for, all by ourselves.

When a relationship is ending, for example, repeating the words "I am a beautiful, passionate, loving, and giving person" can restore precious self-esteem. At work, when pressed to complete a challenging project by the end of the week, you might say, "I am going to get this project completed by Friday." If you're in the process of adopting a healthier lifestyle, you could tell yourself, "I am changing my life for me." The truer your new positive statements are, the less likelihood that your old negative beliefs will continue.

Another tool Martha introduced was a variation of blindman's buff. She blindfolded me and instructed me to wend through an intricate maze, formed with string attached to other strings.

Martha explained that the exercise simulates what life does to all of us: "Life is an unknown path, and no one gives us directions. There are obstacles, we stumble around in the darkness of our lives, and we have to feel our way very carefully."

Darkness—that was something I knew about. I had so many things stored in the blackness of my life—lost marriage, lost dignity, lost hope. My life had so often been a horrible nighttime-in-the-daytime experience, a massive oil spill of the spirit.

So off I went, in total darkness, through the maze, holding on to the strings for dear life. I must have retraced my steps more than once, coming to a place where the strings met at a forty-five-degree angle, or where a string ended at some obstacle. I walked into a yucca plant, stumbled into some bushes, and nearly tripped over a chair. It was very uncomfortable—and a little scary. I knew I had come to that same corner before, touched that same obstacle before. Then I would turn around and go back, trying to find my way without being able to see.

"Your goal is to develop your internal guidance system, and listen to it," Martha said. "It gives us a clear indication about what is right for us. If it's right, we tend to feel good. If it's wrong, we tend to feel bad. If we ignore our internal feelings and do something we know isn't right, we may regret it later. The only way to win our freedom back is to face our situation honestly and—no matter how terrible things may be—continue to act on the heart's calm guidance."

"Everything you need is within you," Koelle added.

I persevered, using all my instincts. I didn't give up, even as I began to feel frustrated that I couldn't get out of the maze. I kept trying to find my way, back and forth and up and down along the strings, but I couldn't find my way with my eyes covered. If a string felt rough or unusual, I immediately tried to find the correct string. And after going in circles, thinking I would never find my way but not wanting to give up, I finally made it to the end.

"You're home!" Koelle said.

"Am I! Hello! That's good."

"I've never seen anyone learn the maze that fast," added Martha. "You did really well."

"You started out asking a lot of questions . . . what do I do . . . how do I do it . . . tell me where to go, and what if there's . . . and toward the end, you were quiet. You were trusting yourself," Koelle told me.

I'm slowly, stubbornly learning that maybe I should do a little more of that. To make it out of the darkness, I have to trust that my internal guidance system will work to move and direct me where I want to be. Our internal guidance system is foolproof—we're the fools when we don't acknowledge what it's telling us.

Next, I would do some "horse therapy." I have always loved horses, and as I looked forward to working with them, I couldn't help but think of one particular horse that will forever hold a special place in my heart.

NUGGETS:

- Intuition will help you clarify things in your life and point you in the right direction. Once you begin to consistently use your intuition, you'll feel more secure in your decisions.
- Trust yourself. Allow your feelings to be one of your deciding factors.
- Live mindfully. Notice any event or circumstance that opens a door or confirms your intuition. Make time for quiet reflection and listen to your heart.

MORE WISDOM FROM MARTHA

Martha suggested another wonderful tool that helped me immensely—and it may help you, too.

- Imagine the perfect person is with you—someone you love, or Jesus, Buddha, or Santa Claus, any great teacher who appeals to your psyche. This person is telling you exactly what you need to hear.

- Write down both sides of the conversation with this individual. Start by describing how you feel, the presence of fear, anger, and other emotions. Ask the questions you need to ask.
- Then become the other person, and answer your questions as that person would in your very best dreams.
- If this resonates with you, try Martha's Challenge Step: Experiment with believing that what your perfect person tells you is actually what God wants you to hear right now.

From: Sarah

To: Koelle

Dearest Koelle,

My friend, if I may call you that, I cannot believe in such a short time I felt so close to you. You are an incredible person, with a superb golden heart and those eyes, wow, a special lady.

Thank you so much for your kindness in teaching me so much. I have so, so much to learn, and learn I will.

I feel you and your work put me on the road to recovery. And I really want to thank you from the bottom of my heart.

With much love to you and huge gratitude.

I am always here in friendship.

Sarah

From: Martha Beck

To: Sarah

You are an indispensable part of God. Ironically, the more we suffer, the more we seem willing to feel that. As the Fake Sheikh episode fades in time, you have slightly less incentive to abandon the earthly illusion and return to the astonishing reality of the soul. Please make sure you do that now, so you never again have to suffer deeply before shifting your perceptions. And finally, below you'll find a poem that I've always loved. It seems there were people who got it—and reached out to tell you so—even in thirteenth-century Persia.

I say my inner lover, why such panic?
We sense there is some sort of spirit that loves birds and animals
    and the ants—perhaps the same one who gave you radiance
    in your mother's womb.
Is it logical you would be walking around entirely orphaned now?
The truth is you turned away yourself, and decided to go into the
    dark alone.
Now you are tangled up in others, and have forgotten what you
    once knew.
That's why everything you do has some weird sense of failure in it.

—Kabir

DIARY ENTRIES

September 15, 2010

I find that as the days of September tumble on, so the hours tick by, and the workload of daily life rises. It is fascinating to be alone in your own life and not have any full-time assistants. I realized that I was working for my staff, that I torpedoed myself around the world for jobs, in order to keep funding the monthly salaries. That tremendous burden of responsibility is thunderous, and no sooner had you managed a month's salaries, when you had to find the next month's salaries. So I was chained to the treadmill, and my life was slipping into my fifty-first year, without a backward glance. How fascinating to be given this enormous gift of freedom. God is God. I am totally in service and deeply, profoundly humbled by universal light. If we could just get out of our own way . . .

September 27, 2010

I had no idea of the workload in filming this docuseries. It is interesting because it is strange to have a camera crew, who are completely impersonal, watching me cry or get emotional or be totally authentic in front of unknown people. It certainly feels so uncomfortable to talk about my innermost feelings and personal thoughts to total strangers.

I am so excited in one way, but the more I come into my right mind, the more I look at the monstrous mistakes made by my ego, self-sabotaging the other side. I am miserable at the mistakes made. I am so sad when I think of how I blew it.

September 30, 2010

I am so excited about Finding Sarah. *It is now my only focus to get myself right, once and for all. I just cannot go on any longer like this. I am riddled with NO self-worth. None.*

19 | *Heather Blaze*

*Life is like horse jumping: you must set high goals,
take high risks, and strive to make every round clear.*

*W*HEN I AM in trouble, I turn to horses for healing.
The first time a horse healed me was when my marriage to Andrew
was in ruins and I was at a desperate physical and emotional ebb.
In November 1993, I was watching the British Grand Prix, a show-
jumping event at Hickstead. I glanced at the screen and became
transfixed. A remarkable horse was in action, a huge gray ballerina

of a horse, clearing each jump with daylight. What stopped me, too, was the rider, a silver-haired man in a green coat who looked a bit like Liam Neeson. He was the rarest of performers: a stylist. He rode with no spurs. There was elegance and ease in his riding, and you could tell by his body that he talked to and listened to his horse—they moved in perfect rhythm. This man was the most intuitive of riders.

I had not ridden for close to five years. I'd lost my feeling for horses, the sort of thing that happens when you stop listening to yourself. Captivated, I wanted to meet this rider. I knew he could teach me, and I knew he could help me retrieve something.

At the time, I had nothing—I had just moved into a small detached house with my two girls—and had no money coming in regularly. Yet on an impulse, I rang up my most loyal and special assistant, Jane Ambler, and asked her to find this man. It took her two days, but she succeeded. The man's name was Robert Splaine, and he ran an equestrian center in Belgooly in County Cork.

That same month I boarded an Aer Lingus flight to Cork. Two hours later I was shaking hands with Robert and his wife, Eileen, at their home in the rich Irish countryside.

From the stables—this sort of rickety old barn—came Heather Blaze, the gray ballerina, and she was a magnificent, beautiful horse, one of the finest mares in Ireland. The relationship between this horse and Robert was like none I have ever witnessed. When she looked at Robert, you could tell she was in love with him and so responsive to his Irish lilt. I watched them together. She flirted with him, tossing her big rabbitlike ears, and played with him, and Robert returned the affection. The greatest-ever love affair between a horse and a rider—this was Heather Blaze and Robert.

I never rode her because she did not want to have anything to do with me—she loved Robert, and Robert only.

I felt very comfortable in Ireland with Robert and Eileen, sitting around the fire and enjoying soda bread and tea. I blended right in with their family of dogs and horses. It all felt very natural and they accepted me like a sister. It took me back to my roots and I began to breathe again. I started traveling to Ireland a lot to visit the Splaines.

The horse business specializes in prodigious ups and downs. One day I saw Robert come into the training ring, leading Heather Blaze, and he had tears in his eyes.

"Robert, what on earth is wrong with you?"

"The people who own Heather Blaze are selling her to a US interest for close to one million dollars. Soon I will be losing her."

For Robert, this was heartbreaking. Heather Blaze was a spectacular mix of talent, heart, and temperament: a horseman could go a lifetime without finding her like. Without his long-eared beauty, Robert could no longer compete at the top international level, and this seemed to me a crime, a waste of brilliance and grace.

"Over my dead body will that horse leave you!"

I had no funds to speak of at the time, but I vowed that I would raise the money we needed to keep Heather Blaze. I had to help Robert; I couldn't let him and Eileen down.

Somehow I raised over three hundred thousand dollars—not a match for the other buyer's purchase price, but enough for a down payment to forestall the sale. It was too thrilling for belief, that I actually owned such a marvelous horse.

"We must keep her," I told Robert, "because I believe you are going to win the Olympic gold for Ireland."

Robert was such a good man; he deserved it.

At the same time, by focusing on Heather Blaze and helping her, I actually started healing my own life.

Heather Blaze was jumping in peak form in 1995, winning with regularity, but I knew that her acid test would be the King George V Gold Cup in July. As the most coveted trophy in England, the King George lured the very best horses from throughout the world; no Irish rider had won it in thirty-five years. Then again, no rider had been riding the likes of Heather Blaze. Before the competition, I walked up to Heather Blaze and whispered in her ear, "Don't be frightened of the planks, because you are owned by Robert. Just for him, because you are not going anywhere. You are safe."

Robert had supreme confidence in his mount that day, and it showed in the first round. Of more than thirty competitors, only five jumped clear—and of those five, Heather Blaze was the quickest, sailing over the fences as though immune to gravity. Her good time allowed her to go last in the jump-off, exactly Robert's plan.

Heather Blaze delivered that clear round, winning the day. The low-key Robert Splaine took off his hat, tipped it to me, and punched it in the air, to celebrate the high point of his career. Ireland had won!

No one knew I owned Heather Blaze, except Robert and myself, so it was amusing that the owner of the show-jumping ring invited me down to present the trophy. I was presenting it to myself; the secret made our feat the more special.

The amazing Heather Blaze continued to win. The more successful Heather became, the more self-healing I felt.

Some six weeks after the King George, Robert qualified for the Olympics in Atlanta—we had our dream. Next was the Dublin Horse Show in Millstreet, the Grand Prix of Ireland. It was raining that day. Heather Blaze did not like rain. As she started to jump, she must have lost her footing on the water jump. Her legs buckled and her forelegs folded beneath her. She fell upon landing and shattered her left foreleg. There was nothing to be done. She had no chance.

Heather Blaze was shot on the spot.

Robert's first reaction was disbelief, then inconsolable grief. It's customary to consult with an injured horse's trainer before putting her down. But there was no way she could have been saved. He touched her one last time.

Robert walked across the ring, his head low. He had ridden Heather Blaze for four years; she was part of his family. Robert never really got over the loss. We could have bred her, but never did.

I had insured Heather Blaze for two million dollars—but the insurance company refused to pay the full amount. What they did pay, I gave to Robert to find a new horse. I wanted to keep him in the international ring. He was such a brilliant horseman—and he didn't deserve what had happened.

In the wake of my own depression over the loss of Heather, I decided to take myself off to Qatar and ride the desert marathon race on a horse called Gal. I asked Robert and my father to fly over and train me.

On the way, Robert stopped in Zurich to see a friend. In the bowels of an indoor show-jumping ring he found a horse named Ballymoss who jumped well. Though a handsome brown Thoroughbred with obvious potential, Ballymoss was a flawed horse—flawed by nature in that he had a hole in his heart and windpipe. Further, he was malnourished.

Robert asked if we should buy him as he was uninsurable, so we did. We nurtured him, and loved him. No sooner had the horse felt loved than he started to jump brilliantly. Not only that, his heart and windpipe healed. Ballymoss become the number-one show jumper in Ireland. We ended up selling Ballymoss, and he spent many years on the international circuit.

One day Robert saw this enormous great thumping stallion with feet as large as soup plates. His name was Bobbu. Robert wanted to buy him, but the owner said, "You don't want him, because he is a tricky customer." Well, we did buy him, and Robert turned him into a champion and trained him for Olympic success.

Bobbu came from the same bloodline as Heather Blaze, sired by King of Diamonds; in fact, he was a cousin of Heather's. Like Heather Blaze, Bobbu became the best jumping horse in all of Ireland.

Bobbu helped Ireland win a string of international honors, and we wanted him to compete in the 2004 Olympics in Greece. But this was not to be.

One afternoon as Bobbu was returned to his stall, Robert noticed that something in his gait was off. A veterinarian was summoned, but an examination found that Bobbu was fine. Still, Robert sensed something was wrong with Bobbu's right leg. Most people would have let him jump anyway, especially since he had passed the veterinarian examination.

The other option was to give Bobbu a special painkiller for horses to numb the pain. The issue of medicating horses has been a chronic source of controversy. Horses, like all animals, occasionally need medication. Horses are born to run, but their muscles get strained and their joints get stiff. Some of the routinely administered horse drugs not only improve their physical well-being, but also enhance their performance. This can be detrimental, though; a horse can literally overdo it, hurt its legs or muscles, or even run itself to death. Robert didn't like to medicate his horses for that reason, and of course he would never administer performance-enhancing drugs. It was Robert's decision to pull Bobbu from competition.

This was a fortunate decision. Had Bobbu gone on to compete in the Olympics for Ireland, he probably would have hurt himself. The ground was so hard and it was so hot, Bobbu would not have survived.

There is a happy ending: By keeping Bobbu out of competition, Robert saved his life. Bobbu turned out to be the number-one breeding stallion in the world for show jumpers. Every morning he wakes up, heads out to the field, and prances happily about. Bolts of energy come off him. He loves to flirt with all the mares. Endlessly delighted, full of himself, Bobbu lives an extraordinary life.

As for Robert, he is known as the finest show-jumping gentleman ever—at least in my eyes. And because of his success, he became the *chef d'équipe* of the Irish show-jumping team. So in the end he did win Olympic gold, but he won it in himself.

As for me, these horses made me feel alive again. In fact, I am never so much alive as when I am mingling among horses, and some days I don't want to be anywhere else on earth.

From: Martha Beck
To: Sarah
Hello dear,
If you allow people who don't know you to define you, you'll be lost forever. There, in one sentence, is the simple truth about all human relationships.

xxx,
Martha

20 | *Horse Power*

If you are frightened of a horse, he will know it. But if you trust him, the horse will know that, too, and he will repay your confidence with his diligence.

I HAVE BEEN RIDING horses since I was very young. So when Martha and Koelle suggested that I do equine therapy, I was excited—and intrigued.

Using horses and other animals as a means of therapy is not a new concept. Animals have helped people cope with trauma and disorders for many years, ranging from assisting people with disabilities and serving as rescue animals in cases of disaster to acting as companions for the aged and bedridden. The warmth of an animal's body, the softness of its coat—the very fact that it is a living thing—provides an opportunity for emotional relief and connection.

The philosophy behind equine therapy begins with the premise that horses are great teachers, possessing an innate wisdom regarding those around them through the energy fields we all share. Horses are prey animals and have survived thousands of years in the wild based on their ability to pick up on the subtle energy of others, especially predators. By nature, horses have a keen sense of awareness and simultaneous presence (being fully present with themselves and others in the moment)—qualities we struggle a lifetime trying to learn. Some who work with horses believe the animals have a "human eye" that looks right into your soul to sense what you are feeling.

Others believe the bond between humans and animals, horses in particular, evolved from an ancient mutual dependence. In ancient times, animals were everything to us: food, shelter, clothing, even spiritual relatives. Only those humans who successfully developed a close understanding of animals and were enmeshed with the natural world managed to survive. I am Celtic through and through, and after studying how Celtic cultures embrace the horse as a spiritual symbol, I have come to believe that a relationship with animals can be transforming, guiding us toward authenticity and a more passionate life. In Celtic tradition, horses are known as *aman cara*—soul friends.

In short, equine therapy helps people deepen their spiritual connections, gain more clarity in their lives, and learn the meaning of living authentically.

The first time I tried equine therapy was during my first visit to Phoenix in June 2010. Koelle told me: "The time spent with the horses is going to be really important for you to focus on trusting yourself again and overcoming your fears. Horses are quite sensitive about picking up on what's really true for us: our body language and our energy. And they're brilliant at teaching people how to set healthy boundaries. I don't know anything that can teach that better than a horse."

Koelle was so right. She brought a horse out to the corral to see if I could get it to follow me. The horse wanted nothing to do with me. It would not follow me. "Why?" I asked Koelle.

"Do you believe in yourself, Sarah?

"No, of course not, I am always failing miserably."

"The horse senses your insecurities, and as long as you project that negative energy, the horse will not follow you."

I, the so-called expert horsewoman, had a lot to learn!

On my second trip to Phoenix, we ventured out to a Big Sky Ranch, a sprawling place nestled in the rolling foothills of the beautiful Sonoran Desert and infused with the peaceful sounds of nature.

As I wandered to the corral, I spied a stallion that was bleeding from his gums. All I knew was that I had to take care of him and do what was best for him. He had clumps of hair stuck in his teeth, and the hair was causing the bleeding. At first, he was angry and frightened as I approached, but as I stroked his neck and talked to him calmly, he stood quietly, with dignity, while I carefully pulled the hair from his gums and teeth. He sensed that I wanted him to be happy. The horse had been a naughty boy, biting the hair off the back of a nearby horse. I knew he'd be at it again, but I did my best to make him as comfortable as possible. Martha loves this story; she says it sums me up perfectly.

There was a horse chosen especially for me—one that had been abused. What a skittish, high-strung guy he was—a big bay horse, reddish-brown with black mane and tail, whose skin shivered as we approached. He looked at me wildly.

The horse had no name that we knew of, so I decided to call him Flea. Years before, on an Easter Sunday, while running in Grenada, I came across a tiny puppy abandoned on the side of the road. He was about six weeks old, scrawny as an old stick, and riddled with fleas. He squinted up at me with brown eyes that seemed full of the light of tragedy. I scooped him up and wrapped him in my handkerchief.

I knew the little fellow was close to death, not only flea ridden but malnourished and worm infested, too. I took him straightaway to a vet and waited six hours for someone to help me.

Eventually, he was cleaned, bathed, soothed, and inoculated against all the nasties that had plagued him. I left him overnight in the care of the vet staff but returned the next day to retrieve him. I named him Flea. The perfect name!

Quarantine laws forbade me from taking Flea home to London, so I stayed on a while until I could find a proper home for him. And I did—with a wonderful, loving woman who would love him as I did.

And so here I was with his namesake, Flea the horse, with his clean, musky smell, the sun dappling his back, and like me, riddled with insecurities and paranoias.

Koelle and I guided Flea into the ring. When you approach a horse in a field, paddock, or arena, you have to walk slowly. Horses have boundaries like we do, and trust issues. At the point your horse raises his head to acknowledge your approach—or walks away—or walks toward you—you have just bumped into his boundaries.

Unlike horses, I was never good at establishing boundaries. I am too trusting, and it gets me in trouble. By boundary, I mean a healthy barrier between you and other people—like a strong gate that you construct in areas of your life with a sign attached that reads STOP, THAT'S NOT ACCEPTED HERE. It's a line in your life, where you have determined that others cannot cross. Boundaries that are clearly defined and defended say things like: "You may not verbally abuse me or invade my space." We have an internal boundary, too—an invisible shield that guards and protects us from verbal hurts. It stops us from automatically taking in or accepting another's hurtful words.

In the ring with Flea I had to gain his trust by showing him that I was the leader. Horses want someone else to lead; they would rather not have that responsibility. When you're working with a horse, it wants to know that you are a capable leader who will not allow harm to come to it.

I was to use my energy to get Flea to walk ahead of me, and at the same time show him that I was in control—the leader of the pack. No riding was involved. Horses are herd animals, and so it's best to lead them from behind. This reminded me that we need to let others take the visible lead as we play an important role behind the scenes.

Thinking that Flea knew I was a horse person, I assumed he'd do exactly as I wanted, so I was surprised that he didn't. He sensed that I was edgy, and he trotted away.

"In their presence you must be still," Koelle said. "They respond negatively to people who are too hyper. Relax your belly. Walk in the spirit that is Sarah."

I shrugged my shoulders and smiled vaguely. I allowed myself a few deep breaths to calm down. It was only when I relaxed and concentrated on the moment that Flea obeyed me. The minute I doubted myself or had some other emotions come up, he hesitated. He knew I was caught up in my ego, and reflected his experience of me.

Then, gently, I went up to him, and in my mind I sent out the message that if he wanted to connect with me, that was okay. Flea sauntered up closer to me, nudged his velvety nostrils at me, and laid his nose on my heart. We made a connection. He picked up on my good energy. Horses teach us how to be sensitive to each other and ourselves simultaneously; it is an incredible gift.

In the deepest sense, you must earn your horse's confidence, his trust, and his love. If you are firm but also gentle, if you are his boss yet his friend, then he will do anything for you within reason, and sometimes beyond.

"The authority you have with horses can't be from anything forced," said Koelle. "It has to be authentic or the horse won't respond. Now, are you ready to take this to the next level?"

"Yes."

Flea had a serious fear of plastic bags, terrified that the bags were going to attack or harm him in some way. I was to help him get over his phobia.

Koelle instructed me to touch Flea with the plastic bags.

"He may jump . . . he may spook. But don't get tangled up in his fear, okay?"

I began to rub him with a plastic bag. He jumped back and ran away. He did this over and over again. It took forever (at least it seemed that way) before Flea got comfortable with the bags.

The key to this work was to remain true and strong to my core—not try to be the savior and take Flea's fears away. It wouldn't work. I was to keep to my center, to show the horse I was not frightened and I trusted him. The horse would sense this and his own fears would dissipate.

Working with Flea helped me tap into my many fears. Fear is a core emotion, a primordial feeling that all animals experience. It's simply a feeling of impending doom, of dread or apprehension about something—fear of failure, of being fat, of being alone, of being broke, fear of losing face, fear of disappointment, rejection, or physical injury.

Usually we run from our fears, like Flea did, repressing or denying them. But this is a very short-term strategy. That's because, emotionally speaking, what we resist persists. Or, to use Henry Miller's more eloquent language, "Everything we shut our eyes to, everything we run away from, everything we deny, denigrate or despise, serves to defeat us in the end."

The best way to overcome fear is what Flea did: Face your fear, again and again. Then simply look at your fear objectively. Usually it's overblown. I ask myself: "Can I deal with the worst-case scenario?" Usually I can; therefore I can call the shots. The second thing that works for me is that when fearful and in doubt, just hang in there. Do what you know is the right thing to do (which automatically means it's going to be the hard way), no matter what.

Flea helped me understand myself better. When you're working with an animal that is bigger than you, you experience yourself in relationship to the animal. You learn to face your fears, set boundaries, and eventually lead the horse. This directly correlates to how you lead your life.

I miss him. Flea was a life-support system cleverly disguised as a horse.

NUGGETS:

- Tap into the healing power of animals in your life. Volunteer at a humane society or rescue organization. Walk the dogs, or cuddle the cats.
- Take an animal vacation where you can have supervised close encounters with horses, dolphins, or other animals. Or be an appreciative spectator. Go to a horse show, for example. The sheer beauty of these incredible creatures that are so full of energy and strength and passion can take us out of our own egos.
- Set clear boundaries in your life.
- Be open. When you are welcoming, others will be drawn to you and will feel at ease in your presence. They will want to approach you, get to know you, and/or spend time with you.
- Face your fears (which, by the way, is the only way to conquer them!). The universal law of nonresistance says that when you face your fears head-on, they'll fall away of their own weight. So take a deep breath and strap on your scuba gear, board that plane, apologize to your ex-friend, or do whatever it is that you're afraid of, before this year is over.

DIARY ENTRIES

October 4, 2010

Life is getting better. I have to continue to change the past, the negative rut that is endlessly taking me from the good rut.

I have to get my good rut.

"I love myself more than I ever imagined possible and

others love me too." This is a mantra I write twenty-five times a day . . . or more, and certainly say it.

I look at Andrew, who is growing from strength to strength. I am always with him, but feel like he is ready to fly now.

In writing this, I have tears again, just mourning and grieving the past. Why did I get it so wrong?

I look at the green tree through the window and see the weather turn to autumn. The change of seasons means that life does not stop for anyone, and time continues, with or without you. So if I just trust and allow, then, maybe, like the seasons, I, too, will be directed and change. God is the conductor.

October 8, 2010

I recently declined a dinner invitation with a couple. They got cross, annoyed, and are not talking to me. Why? I did not want to go; I wanted to be quiet. Should I not follow what I wish to do in order to please others? I have done this all my life.

Somehow I need to toughen up. Or do it?

From: Martha Beck

To: Sarah

There are three kinds of business in this world: your business, my business, and God's business. Doing what you feel is right, making space for yourself, and setting boundaries that allow you to thrive—all those actions are your business. How people choose to interpret your boundaries, whether or not they try to make you feel bad, whether or

not they continue to speak to you—that's their business. YOU CAN-
NOT CONTROL OTHER HUMAN BEINGS. That means you CAN'T
make them feel anything they choose not to. You can't make some-
one happy, you can't make someone angry, you can't make someone
afraid. They do that by deciding how they'll interpret your actions and
everything else. You can make things more likely but never certain.

No one can make you miserable either. You decide what pain or
happiness you create in yourself, by choosing how to interpret other
people's actions, and the world in general. When you decide to believe
that people are punishing you, you're mentally punishing yourself and
them. This creates a cycle of negativity wherein you catalyze as much
punishment as possible for yourself and others.

You really can be the master creator of all your own circumstances.

xoxox,
M

DIARY ENTRIES

October 15, 2010
Dear Diary,
I am back writing again. As I sit down to recap on an ex-
traordinary week, I ask myself, "Where shall I start this
entry?" At this very moment, my trusted and special little
Lee and I are on a train, from Stoke-on-Trent to London.
We're actually going in the right direction. That's a miracle
for me, since my lovely Lee and I normally head off thinking
the other knows where we are going!

Lee has been with me for 26 years. She is from the East
End of London, and her father drives a black cab. Lee travels

with me, looks after me, and is also my hairdresser. For the last 13 years, we've been all over the world together.

As the train passes through the British countryside, the sun is shining down on the leftovers from last night's frost, and the ground is twinkling. The scene reminds me of one big John Constable painting. Constable was a famous English romantic painter in the 1800s whose landscape paintings of ordinary English life are now among the most popular and valuable in British art.

As I look out, there are cows in the field, there are barge owners chatting as the steam rises from their coffee cups. I sit back in wonder. This is England at its best. I am proud to be British.

I have always loved traveling by train. *The Railway Children* was probably the catalyst for this love.

Looking at life through the windows of a train is like watching a cinema. Scenes and snapshots of real life go by quickly, frame by frame, seen through my window. I study every view, every tree, and imagine the stories behind them. I love my trains and my window cinema—and their ever-changing pictures.

Last night, I attended the birthday party of my dear friend John Caudwell in Stoke-on-Trent. This is the land of Lord Wedgwood, home to the famed pottery factories of good old-fashioned Britain. I knew very few people and walked in on my own. I was completely happy and felt good. A kind couple, Beverley and Peter from Essex, came up for a chat, worried that I would be feeling lonely or self-conscious. It was extremely kind of two strangers; however, I was having a good time with Sarah!

Then the photographs started, and many people wanted a snapshot of me and them. I was touched and heartened they wanted them, and when someone said, "Does this annoy you?" I heard myself say, "It is indeed a very kind and nice gesture of them to want a photograph with me. Their kindness in wanting one restored my faith in myself."

My best friend Clare's stepfather's memorial service was at 12 noon. I walked into the church, and Clare seated me with her family. I felt the arms of love and care. Clare's mum, Annie, had adopted me as her own daughter when I was 8 years old. Here was this fine, beautiful lady, racked with sadness and grief yet again. She had endured so many losses: her first husband, Anthony, to cancer; her grandson (Clare's son) to suicide at only 21; and now another beloved husband, Peter, to cancer. The service was so moving, and I was pushed to tears by the bravery and courage of Clare and her whole family.

Afterward, I spotted many of my father and mother's best friends: Patrick, my special and devoted godfather, and Sarah, my mum's bestest friend. She reached out her arms with love and shouted "Hello, Fergie!" with so much joy in her voice. She must be about 75 years old and she looked like the friend I remember Mum loving so much all those years ago. And yes, you guessed it, here came the tears—nostalgic tears that touched my heart.

I was sitting in the same house where all those years ago my mother dropped me off to play with Clare. And today, there were so many people genuinely happy to see Fergie. Their embrace showed me so much. The universe is shining *light daily for me now, on the past, present, and future. It is embracing me, and I am trusting the light to guide me. Clare summed it up best by saying, "Thank heavens, I have my old friend Fergie back."*

I left quickly, because I felt my tears were now becoming uncontrollable. Too difficult to handle. As I returned to Royal Lodge, I realized that I was, at long last, being completely authentic and real to my feelings, and just maybe, I was mourning the death of my mother, my father, and looking at the happiness of my life as a child, and mourning all that too. It triggered a massive eruption of emotion, and I am glad for it. In hindsight, it has to be said: Thanks to the News of The World, I have woken up and looked properly at my life. I am now living it, not running through it, rushing to the next station like a train!

It is October 15. My birthday. I am 51 years old. I woke up sporting a brand-new pair of tartan pajamas. Luckily no man in sight!

Beatrice and Eugenie organized a birthday party for me, and 26 people came to dinner. Again—what a show of generosity and immense kindness. My daughters' love, devotion, and complete unconditional selflessness to want their mother celebrated are beyond any words that I could say.

October 20, 2010

I look at my Ex, and how great he is becoming, more and more centered within himself. He is blossoming into the man I knew he was when I married him. I keep thinking, why did we get divorced? In hindsight, I would say to any-

one who takes impulsive, spontaneous giant steps, fighting for a change within a marriage, never be impulsive, because it might be irrevocable. I live in the grasps of the tentacles of regret.

From: Clare
To: Sarah
My friend,
Regrets are a waste of energy. They eat you up and get in the way of enjoying the present. We all have regrets, but there is nothing we can do about missed opportunities or mistakes in the past. The best we can do is recognize our mistakes and not repeat them.

Look in the mirror and see the Fergie of today—not the one you are angry with, but the one who has a bigger understanding of life than most. Smile at her and tell her you love her. You are VERY SPECIAL and very loved.

xxxxxx
Clare

21 | *Bent but Not Broken*

The good times and the bad times have made me the woman I am today, and I have nothing to regret about that.

THOUGH NOW GRATEFULLY debt free, I had been embroiled in a financial crisis that was, of course, of my own making. You see, I tumbled headlong into serious debt following the collapse of a company I formed several years ago. I was advised time and again to file for bankruptcy, but stubbornly, if not foolishly, I did not want to do so, because I was trying so hard to protect all the people working for me. I had promised them their jobs were secure.

My problem, of course, was that I no longer had any assets to back up such a promise. I worked hard to earn what money I needed, but being in a deep hole, I had a steep climb ahead. With threats and lawsuits swirling around me on a daily basis, I searched for the kind of situation that would fill the coffers more quickly—but ultimately led to my undoing.

By 2010, my money was running out, and I wasn't sure how to pay for daily living, never mind dig myself out of my landslide of debt. The reality of having no money really hit me. I felt desperate.

I never, ever, had to be grown-up about money. As a newlywed, I came into Buckingham Palace with a bank overdraft of $800—a serious sum when you are making $18,000 a year and your sole asset is a ten-year-old car.

You might think that by marrying into the Royal Family my money worries would be over, that I would live solvently ever after in the bosom of one of the richest families in the world.

The reality was something different. For I had married the second son and that made all the difference. Although Andrew received a moderate sum from the Civil List, it went for the cost of civil engagements and for staff and office expenses. In all our years together, his annual income never exceeded fifty thousand dollars.

In all fairness to myself, I was not entirely insouciant about my growing pool of red ink back then. I tried to save money where I could. I found that some designers would allow me a deep discount in return for the publicity value of my wearing their fashions. Unfortunately, this was completely misinterpreted by the tabloids. I was labeled "Freebie Fergie" although I was merely trying to be frugal! I should have been called "Frugal Fergie."

What everyone failed to understand was that I urgently wanted to work, to earn, to be productive. I always loved working, and I missed a real job's stimulation and rested uneasy in depending upon the Royal Family. I had been on my own since the age of eighteen, and I liked how it felt to pay my own freight. I needed some productive, stimulating work.

It came in the form of an idea for my first children's book—born at five thousand feet. I had been taking lessons to learn how to fly a helicopter. By 1987 I had grown bored with my lessons, so I turned them into a childish adventure playground. I started calling my helicopter "Budgie" after the bird I thought it resembled. Before long I had infused Budgie with a full-fledged personality and I was scribbling out plot lines. In October 1989 my first two children's books—*Budgie the Little Helicopter* and *Budgie at Bendick's Point*—came out.

Budgie led to a wonderfully satisfying career as a children's book author in which I created a host of colorful, lovable characters. One of my favorites is Little Red—a red-haired little girl that I first sketched on a paper napkin as a logo for my American charity, Chances for Children. It was turned into a doll as a fund-raising project for P. J., the young boy who was burned over 62 percent of his body during the Oklahoma City bombing. There was no one to pay his medical bills, so Chances for Children pitched in.

Then, on Sept. 11, 2001, a firefighter pulled a Little Red doll from the rubble of the World Trade Center, where Chances for Children had its offices. That little sign of hope amid such inconceivable tragedy and devastation prompted me to expand Little Red's reach all the way to raising funds for a day school in Kabul, Afghanistan, which 1,500 students now attend. To me, Little Red represents the strong, confident, and kind little girl I wished I had been as a child. In the spring of 2011, I visited Ground Zero and donated the original Little Red to the museum, scheduled to open on September 11, 2011.

All of my children's books led me to feel blessed that I was able to put them to work for charities that are close to my heart.

Now back to my money problems: When Andrew and I decided to make our divorce final, I opted for friendship, not money, from the Royal Family. Her Majesty asked me, "What do you require, Sarah?" and I said, "Your friendship," which I think amazed her, because everyone said I would demand a big settlement. But I wanted to be able to say, "Her Majesty is my friend," not fight her or have lawyers saying, "Look, she is greedy." I left my marriage knowing I'd have to work. And I did.

But as a single mother with few assets and less income than most presumed, I found myself in deep financial trouble and struggling with life in the real world. My bank balance remained somewhat precarious until need and opportunity converged during a single serendipitous event.

Howard J. Rubenstein, a New York public relations consultant who coincidentally represented both me and Weight Watchers, invited me and Al Lippert, the founder of Weight Watchers, to a dinner party. I had recently slimmed down by more than fifty pounds from the 203 pounds that earned me the stinging "Duchess of Pork" label from the British press. Everything clicked. I was offered, and later signed, a one-year contract with executives of the H. J. Heinz Company, Weight Watchers' owner. One of those executives was Sir Anthony O'Reilly, Heinz's Dublin-born former CEO.

It could not have come at a better time. Sir Anthony and Howard saved my life. There's no question about it. I would jump off a bridge for them. I really would.

I ended up working for Weight Watchers for twelve proud years. The position gave me discipline in my life and helped me reverse my desperate financial situation. Of course I was widely and unfairly criticized in Britain for it all, when in truth I was just a simple single mother with a love for her work, an entrepreneur, trying to make ends meet.

Unfortunately, I continued to spend money to help other people. I donated every penny I could to charity. I enjoyed my money by using it to ease the plight of others, and I had no conception of how damaging to my own life that would be. Looking back, I see this as another form of people-pleasing—the same behavioral pattern, only in a different design. I was generous to a fault.

Even so, I plodded into the future, still spending money and helping people with their finances. Had I overcome these habits back then, I would not have been in the sorry financial position I found myself in by 2010. There I was again, in middle age, in chronic terror, and in the same predicament, only worse. Instead of building a life, I was living in a rut, in debt, with no money to speak of.

Where had the money gone *this time*?

My slow drift into insolvency stemmed from the collapse of my company, Hartmoor, which I'd set up in 2006. Located in an office building on Madison Avenue in Manhattan, Hartmoor was intended as a vehicle to market my career in publishing, media, and public speaking. I funneled $1.4 million of my own savings into the business, including earnings from producing the film *The Young Victoria* and profits from my children's books. A percentage of sales was set to go to the Sarah Ferguson Foundation. I had great hopes when Hartmoor launched, chirping to an interviewer that I intended it to be "a global inspirational lifestyle and wellness company."

Although I owned 51 percent of Hartmoor, I had partners whom I trusted to manage the business, but we weren't successful. Hartmoor incurred expenses that were far greater than the revenue it generated. There were high-priced salaries to pay, pricey offices to maintain. The debts were rising faster than floodwater through a broken levee. I protested, but no one would listen to my pleas to manage the company with better fiscal responsibility.

Hartmoor's struggles coincided with the end of my contract with Weight Watchers in 2008. In the end, Hartmoor was a loser and ceased operating in May 2008. I took out a $1.7 million personal loan to repay creditors, and in return regained the rights to my own name. The upshot of my legal wrangling was a bill of more than $1.4 million.

By June 2010, I was on the brink of bankruptcy, with barely

nine hundred dollars to my name. I found myself living the same nightmare my mother had endured at the end of her life, and I was terrified that I'd become just like her.

To save myself financially, I looked and looked and looked for help but to no avail. I was bent and about to break. I realized after the Fake Sheikh incident that I had been on a treadmill, walking fast to nowhere. For many years, I had worked flat out to pay the salaries for my special and loyal staff, many of whom stayed in the trenches and mopped up my tears.

A call came in from the Duke's office: "If you wish to have financial help from the Duke, you will have to make your staff redundant." I felt desperate. I had no choice but to accept the offer and lay off my staff. I was finished, washed up. I surrendered.

The last person to drive off was Helen Jones, who for years had stayed by my side, casting a watchful eye over me, always making my life better. She gave me all her love and care, energy and light. Now she was gone. I had let her and everyone else down. All of these emotions fueled my self-hatred.

I needed to understand what drives my behavior when it comes to money—what money means to me, what it signifies about me, how it makes me feel when I spend or save it. That would be a key to my well-being, financial and otherwise. I had to stop committing financial suicide.

My guide on this part of my journey was Suze Orman, the tough-talking financial guru seen every week by millions on television. She and her partner K.T. arrived by black cab at Royal Lodge to meet with me.

I gave them a quick tour of the Lodge and its grounds. When I showed Suze my bedroom, she was taken aback by all the cuddly stuffed animals I have on my bed.

"You've got to get rid of all those toys. That is childlike, and you shouldn't be a child anymore," she said.

I just laughed it off, with no intention of clearing the bed of my lovely stuffed animals. Suze did like the fact that I am fond of Ganesh, the Hindu god who is the remover of obstacles. She is as well, and she liked the fact that I have a lot of Ganeshes around my home.

As we chatted on about my financial issues, Suze had a big "aha" moment: "You don't have a money problem; you have a self-worth problem. Your so-called money problem comes from buying approval from everyone."

Suze Orman proclaiming that I had no money problem was, well, revelatory—and it certainly lightened my load. But, of course, she was right: My own feelings of lack of worth had precipitated my overspending on friends and family. Suze helped me see how self-worth issues were the engine that pulled the train of my financial problems.

The three of us bonded immediately, and I knew I had made two new friends.

We met again in New York City and got down to business at warp speed.

"After the scandal broke, no one wanted to employ you, right? And all income stopped?" Suze asked.

"Correct."

"And Prince Andrew stepped in to save the day?"

As I mentioned earlier, Andrew rescued me with his own money and helped me sidestep bankruptcy proceedings. We sent letters to my creditors, boldly offering them a quarter of what they were owed. They helped me restructure my debt.

Suze bored in. "What does it feel like to be dependent?"

"If I didn't have Andrew, I'd be homeless," I said haltingly.

"You need to make money. You need to be independent. But success comes one project at a time. So we need a strategy."

I outlined for Suze the projects I was hatching to help me get back on my financial feet, including doing television work, going on a speaking circuit, and turning my Little Red children's books into a series of cartoons.

"There's your money strategy," Suze nodded. "But you must also have a personal strategy. Although a better net worth can make life less stressful, it won't help with your self-worth."

Suze wanted to dredge up the scandal. But I didn't want to go there. It was quite beside the point now, like an artifact looted from an ancient grave, an oddly shaped tool no longer of any use. I wanted to move forward, using the experience as an opportunity to learn. I wanted to master the lesson and find the greatest treasure of all—a "me" I'm proud of.

So I asked Suze, "How do I find self-worth?"

"There isn't one key that gives you self-worth. It's not one-dimensional."

At that point I wished Suze could wave a financial magic wand and make everything better. But it wasn't that easy.

"Girlfriend, you need to turn your attitude around before we even start working on your financial situation," Suze advised. "Thinking that you're not good enough has been preventing you from loving yourself, being true to yourself, and doing what you really want to do in your life. It's making you feel as if you don't measure up. It's also leading you to align your everyday behaviors and choices with what you think others want and expect from you. That's why you've got money problems!

"I want you to start appreciating how amazing you are. That's your personal strategy. Now is the time to focus on the positive rather than the negative. You're not on the street; you're not starving. You have wonderful daughters and a great life ahead of you. I know it feels as if starting over at fifty-one is late, but you have one of the most important possessions: the courage to change."

Suze grilled me aggressively, and I'm glad she did. Changing my habits would be tough, but I felt I was headed in the right direction.

I wrote in my diary:

_____

I had a great time with Suze Orman. Suze asked me my most terrifying fear. I responded that it was the fear of never knowing or loving myself. Suze assured me that I would eventually find Sarah.

The more I come into my right mind, the more I look at the monstrous mistakes made by my ego, which sabotaged my life. I'm terribly sad about the mistakes made.

I'm so miserable at what the past is telling me, and the shame and humiliation of letting so many down. It feels catastrophic to live with.

At least I have my girls. We have a magical circle of love for each other that is never-ending.

_____

With Suze's guidance, I faced up to what I owed, to really see the numbers and not merely slide them under my accountant's rug. Suze feels that most people are unhappy because they aren't being honest with themselves, especially about money and finances.

"Being truthful with yourself plugs you into your inner power. You aren't going to be content or successful until you are connected to your heart and operating with all your energy. And that requires a commitment to a life based on honesty in every aspect."

Martha Beck chimed in via email with some advice all of us can use:

> *Your areas of fuzziness are mainly exaggerations or lack of specificity around money. I'm not sure you know how much you have, where it goes, and how it comes in. I hate tracking numbers myself, so I more than understand this, but I think getting incredibly, scientifically honest about money is the fastest way for you to extricate yourself from the quicksand that's trying to swallow you.*
>
> *Are you willing to take this challenge? It means you can only say things about money that you actually know to be true. For instance, instead of, "I have nothing," you'd specify what you do have, which would require your actually KNOWING how much you have, which would require some research. It won't be easy, but at some point, it's going to be necessary, sooner or later. You decide.*

I decided I didn't want to worry about money. I didn't want to be chasing my bills. I focused on paying off my credit-card balances. But mainly I needed to keep my people-pleasing money habits in check. Subconsciously, I had believed I was buying people's affection, but I usually got nothing meaningful in return. So I'd filled that hole by spending money, and then I'd feel terribly guilty. I deserved to treat myself better than that.

If any of us "buys" approval, the next thing we know, we're in debt, we're unhappy with what we have, or we develop an even more insatiable need to people-please. I had to see money for what it is—a way to buy necessities, not as a way to buy my way into someone's heart.

I'm keeping track of my expenses, tallying every last dime, something I've never done because I trusted others to do it for me.

It's duller than eating plain porridge for breakfast, but it taught me why and how my cash was leaking away.

Before, I had been out of touch with my money, then out of touch with my life—a place no one wants to be. Now, I had to sit down and create a realistic estimate of what I spend on average each month, and take into consideration costs for vacations and social events.

I went on a mostly cash diet. It's a known law of financial physics: Plastic attracts debt. So I stopped using all my credit cards (except one, for emergencies), and when I buy, I spend actual money.

Also, I visualized my life without money worries, when I'd be able to use my money for some interesting or more important things.

Whether it's the result of the bad economy, losing a job, or being ill prepared for a catastrophe, so many people are facing serious money problems. I know what it's like to be seriously in debt, and I want to give you hope. You can take control of your finances. When you do, I guarantee you'll reap more than monetary rewards: You'll relieve so much stress, you won't know what to do with all that freed-up space in your mind and heart. You might even enjoy your life more.

NUGGETS:

- Take charge of your finances, and you will take charge of your life.
- Manage your own money. It's fine to surround yourself with a team of money advisors, but you should make the decisions.
- Pay attention to what you have coming in, how much is going out, and where it is going.

- Erase the idea of "lack" from your mind. The feeling that we need money is to focus on the lack of it, and that prevents us from receiving it.
- Stay grateful, and show it by giving back to your community and to organizations you believe in.
- Overspending comes from people-pleasing or from an addiction to seeking approval from others. I always seem to get this one wrong—so who am I to give guidance here?—but this is what I'm trying to learn myself.

From: Suze Orman

To: Sarah

Truth always resonates with the heart and soul. And it is always the right time to hear and feel the truth. It really is that simple, Dear One. It is when the soul merges with itself—it is when you love the mere fact that who you are totally fulfills who you want to be—then being alone is a state of celebration, not a state of loneliness—my wish for you my Dear Duchess is that from this day forward you truly celebrate every breath that you take and every moment you get to spend alone.

From: Martha Beck

To: Sarah

Hi dear,

Here's the key: Always be true to your own ethos. Decide what you believe to be moral and responsible behavior, and live that way.

You've talked to me before about how you feel trapped and smothered because your openness and high spirits aren't considered the ideal "stiff upper lip" mode for someone in your position. Well, trying to force yourself into a personality that wasn't you is what I believe led to things like the Fake Sheikh. You CANNOT live according to rules that violate your essential self. Better, by far, to live openly and calmly according to your best version of human behavior. Someone can always find fault with you—that's not your business. Your business is to live honestly, to be your true self. Then at least when someone finds fault, you'll know that it's simply an honest disagreement.

My experience shows that people who live this way outlast media storms and rise above them. Those who pander to anyone and everyone's code, desperate for approval and affirmation, end up selling themselves down the river. (That idiom is an old reference to slavery, by the way. You aren't anyone's slave. Don't behave like one.)

I know this must be so frightening, but you are up to it. You're working with good people. All is well, and all will be well, and all manner of things will be well.

22 | *No Mission Impossible*

The role of mothers in any community is enormously important. They look after the health of the family—where vaccinations are available, they make sure their children have them, for example—and in many countries they provide the household income. There is no doubt that women do most of the world's work.

$\mathcal{T}$HE ONLY PLACE I feel at home is away from home, working by the side of children who are ill or have been callously cast aside. It's in my heart, working with children. God has just placed a burning desire within me to help develop better oppor-

tunities for them. Over the past fifteen years, I've used funds from my commercial work and my charity, Children in Crisis, to help care for children with AIDS and build schools for deprived children in Africa.

Several years ago, against the advice of many, I went to the small war-ravaged West African nation of Sierra Leone, where my charity Children in Crisis was at work rebuilding schools. Sierra Leone is one of the poorest nations on earth despite the fact that it is home to diamond mines that have produced some of the world's extraordinary stones. If you are familiar with the term "blood diamonds," you know it refers to a savage decade-long civil war in Sierra Leone that virtually destroyed its entire society. It was a war that divided the country, turning neighbor against neighbor and unleashing packs of youth rebels responsible for murdering and maiming millions. Ironically, the war was funded from the sale of diamonds. Visit Sierra Leone today and you will be outraged, not only by the country's poverty and poor infrastructure, but by the common sight of people of all ages who are missing limbs. This is because the civil war was fought using violence and terror. Rebels wielding machetes would systematically attack people in their villages, hacking off hands, arms, and legs of men, women, and children. Those who did not die of their wounds became walking reminders of who was in control.

I spent an afternoon with a young crippled boy named Mohammed, a victim of the horrors of civil war there. He raised his hand and pointed to a boy his age playing on a makeshift soccer field. Then Mohammed touched the stump of his upper leg cut off at the knee.

"That boy out there was my best friend before the war. He was forced into the rebels' army and one night he came to me high on drugs and so out of his mind that he took my leg off. I forgave. I am stronger by my willingness to forgive and move on."

It is from children like Mohammed that I draw profound inspiration and courage.

Thankfully, the war ended, and Sierra Leone is now rebuilding itself very slowly with the help of the international community. Children in Crisis, working in conjunction with other charities, has refurbished or rebuilt eight schoolhouses, making this the first generation in nearly fifteen years to have any access to education. I cannot tell you how deeply touching it is to see these children in the classroom, many of them maimed and united as survivors— behaving much as the children at your or my child's school. These children feel privileged to be alive, let alone in school. They are happy and inquisitive and exceedingly gentle and kind toward each other.

Now Sierra Leone is one nation again. Gone are the brutal attacks on innocent people. It will take a long time before trust is restored, which makes the children of Sierra Leone so important. Many have been spared the emotional trauma suffered by children who lived through the worst violence. The country's best chance at getting back on its feet is the young children of today, who see themselves as belonging to Sierra Leone, as well as belonging to their tribe, village, community, school, and family. Indeed, the greatest "gross national product" for any nation is its youth, and as adults I feel we are responsible for giving children a future.

While on my journey to find Sarah, I was asked to find funds to help save a baby's life—seven-month-old baby Daniel from Colombia. He suffered from a rare liver disease called biliary atresia, a blockage in the tubes (ducts) that carry bile from the liver to the gallbladder. The condition is congenital, which means it is present from birth. The only two treatments for this disease are the Kasai procedure, which baby Daniel had gone through already, and a liver transplant, which baby Daniel needed, or else he would die. The estimated cost of the transplant was $350,000 to $400,000.

Baby Daniel's parents had raised nearly $90,000 on their own. I contacted various charities in my children's charity network, and they responded. Intense media attention raised awareness, and donations came in from everywhere. Baby Daniel had his liver transplant and it was very successful. It breaks my heart to see children who are suffering; I can't stand by and watch it. I have to get involved, always.

This type of work is not for everyone, but it is for me, despite the heartbreaking stories I have faced—like the boy who lay on his back in an Eastern European orphanage but often crawled to the window to feel a patch of sunlight on his face. Or the small boy Max who was kept in a large box in another orphanage.

Sometimes I have flashbacks of a brutal, soul-draining trip I made in 2008 to Romania. I went there with my daughters to visit orphanages rumored to be living hellholes of abuse and neglect.

Beatrice accompanied me to an orphanage in Bucharest. Many children there were tied to benches like dogs. Beatrice angrily asked the head nurse why the children were tied up. Muttering unhappily, the nurse started to untie them; she clearly knew it was wrong.

I then demanded that an emaciated teenage girl be untied. The nurse bowed to the pressure but before she had a chance to act, I impatiently jumped in and began releasing the girl myself. It's just the way I am. Could be the Celtic redheaded Irish in me, I don't know, but all I do know is if I was lying in that bed and I knew there was a big old battle-ax like me out there shouting for me, I'd be pretty pleased.

People might criticize my spontaneity. Honestly, do you think an orphan in there minds if I'm spontaneous? All that child wants is somebody to be their champion.

Perhaps most disturbing of all was the repetitive behavior displayed by so many of the children, the all-too-common sign of complete neglect. Every corner we turned, we found children endlessly rocking back and forth. Some of them rocked backward and forward, some of them rubbed their hands and studied their fingers, some of them simply scratched until they bled. No one did anything for them. Some had sores on their skin where wounds had become infected for want of basic hygiene.

I went there as a mum, and I went because those children are silent whispers. I had to be their voice and bring attention to the deplorable conditions. Still, thousands and thousands of children around the world are in desperate need. Imagining the need can be paralyzing, but just to know that I may have helped in some way makes me realize how much good can come from the work of just a few people.

Perhaps there are some who think I am just some ex-Royal dipping her toes in charity work, but when I see something that needs help then I act, especially when it involves children. I do it because I want to, not because I feel I should. I don't want to do magazine shoots of me holding abandoned babies. This isn't about me—it's about what I can do. I have always wanted to make a difference.

But I have to confess that in the aftermath of the Fake Sheikh scandal, I knew that I had lost track of important things in my life. I felt empty. In that emptiness, it didn't seem to matter what I did. Between doing nothing and doing something, it seemed better to do something. I needed to refocus my attention and my energies.

I knew I had to come out of the corner, be who I was meant to be, and continue to stand up with courage for what I know is right. I needed a kick in the backside to get back on the public stage and be true to myself.

Which is why I sought the help of Stedman Graham.

Stedman is a speaker who teaches identity leadership development, education, and is a bestselling author. He exudes so much passion and confidence.

"Do you have a personal identity?" he asked me.

I shuddered a bit. That's because I equate identities with a group of management types sitting down in a room and sweating bullets until they can come up with a company mission statement that is so long, complicated, and overly far-reaching that it will please the boss and the consultant hired to shepherd the mission-writing process.

Stedman explained that having an identity has nothing to do

with becoming the predominant anything, or climbing the ladder of success or of society. It describes, simply, in a few well-chosen words, your purpose in life.

"An identity is a foundation on which to build your future aspirations and an internal guide for everyday living. If you get lost, distracted, or pulled toward another direction, your personal identity serves as your internal compass to keep you centered and focused on your objective."

As Stedman talked, I thought about this for a while and realized that I do indeed have my own identity. It can be negative or positive—I've just never thought of it in those terms.

I began to ask myself some key questions: Am I doing the work that I will be proud of when I am lying on my deathbed looking back at my life? Am I using my experience and my gifts in the most meaningful way possible? How am I affecting the lives of people around me? Am I being true to my beliefs, my values, and my personal integrity? Am I truly happy doing the work I am doing? What else could I be doing?

In some quiet, contemplative moments, I looked at where I had experienced the most joy. I have always believed that I best experience happiness in my work with children. I asked myself to focus on the occasions when I was most passionate about my work, and I recognized that it was when I was mindfully listening to and helping forgotten children. It was when I looked into their eyes and knew that I could walk that journey with them so they need not be alone. It was when I could provide a quiet presence to help them find some peace and comfort.

As a result of that soul-probing work, my personal mission statement boiled down to this: *Educate and support mothers to keep them from abandoning their children.*

During my many years of working with children, I've become convinced that the mother is the CEO of the family, its heart, and its cornerstone. Mothers run their homes and family in the same way a chief executive runs a business empire. Yet mothering is one of those "professions" in which the majority of those entering it have not had years or months in a school—or even basic boot camp—to develop their skills. Shortly after the first child arrives, a mom finds she has a job much more complex than she could possibly have imagined. Because mothers are the first educators of children, an uneducated and unskilled mother will pass on the same to her child. Mothers are on the front lines when it comes to raising a child on a day-to-day basis. They need support and education.

Over the last three years, I've been developing a program called the Mothers' Army. Internet based, it would be a social network, connecting mothers all over the world with resources, educational materials, support, and encouragement. Mothers would be empowered to make choices that are best for them and their children. A mother in Pakistan, for instance, could connect with a mother in France for help with parenting and child-rearing. I see the Mothers' Army as a natural extension of the work I've done with children up to now. The Mothers' Army would mark the fulfillment of my mission.

I believe we can all benefit from having a personal mission. Set aside some quiet time to consider what's important to you and then let those answers guide you as you answer the following questions: What would you like others to remember about you? What do you want others to experience when they come in contact with you? How will you contribute to the betterment of your community or society at large?

"You have to know who you are, and then you have to organize all the things that you want to achieve in your life, all the things that you are passionate about," Stedman said.

Take time to find out what you really want to do with your life. Creating a personal mission statement defines your purpose on this earth. And it has a powerful effect on how you run your life.

NUGGETS:

- You are on this planet for a reason. Develop a clear vision, lock into your purpose and passion, and set goals with deadlines.
- Answer central questions of your life, and you'll find your mission: What would a meaningful life look like? Where is the pain I can ease? What am I called to do? What tools do I have to accomplish these goals?
- Look inside. We cannot find our mission until we know ourselves. What we think about ourselves is reflected in what we

say and do—in our work, our surroundings, our family life, and our service to others. Therefore, it's important to take the time to get a clearer picture of who we really are.

- Stand up for what you believe. Nothing drains energy more than suppressing action, passion, and commitment.
- Don't be afraid to make changes in your life. If your heart tells you it's right for you, then it's probably the detour you were meant to take. For me, my own truth is to speak out for those who don't have a voice.

From: Lisa
To: Sarah
Dear Sarah,
Thank you for everything that you are doing to help baby Daniel. Thank you again for being there for this sick infant, especially at a difficult time for you,
If ever I can do anything to help in any way—

Love and best wishes,
Lisa

From: Martin
To: Sarah
Your heart has two sides: The smile of a child and the needs of a nation. You are driven to make a difference. You have the energy, passion, and power to make a huge difference in this world, and have done so for more than 25 years.

23 | *Rejuvenation*

We have the power to choose where we fly,
and how high.

HERE I WAS, seated at a long, sleek conference table among a phalanx of sharply dressed legal eagles in the law offices of my attorney, in Beverly Hills. In walked a nurse, Sonya, carrying a little nurse's bag that reminded me of the one I had as child. Except this time, Sonya, a real nurse, was dressed in the nurse's outfit, not me, and ready to take my blood.

I offered up my left arm. Sonya donned protective gloves, put a tourniquet around my arm, and swabbed my inner elbow with an antiseptic solution. With a few words of comfort—"Relax, take a big, deep breath, honey"—she inserted a sterile needle into my vein. A few people in the room almost fainted at the sight of the needle. I was fine, but I wasn't sure that this particular law firm had seen these sorts of shenanigans.

Within moments, deep red blood filled vial after vial. She labeled them and fitted them into a special basket where they stood at attention like good little military officers. Mine, I'm guessing, were among hundreds of similar vials that were taken that day and would be tested for myriad possible maladies.

Sonya said I was a good patient, so she covered my small wound with a sticker that said "Well done!"

I then turned my attention back to the business at hand. Everyone's faces were drained of blood, except mine.

My day was so full that the only time the blood could be drawn was during that meeting. The blood test was performed at the urging of my dear friend, Robin McGraw, the beautiful, vivacious wife of Dr. Phil. Robin is goodness, gentleness, and compassion all wrapped up in one very special human being. Robin is a great advocate for women's health and a living testament of healthy living, so when she suggested that I have a complete physical workup, I agreed. But I was busy with meetings, so Robin arranged for the nurse to draw my blood at my attorney's office.

Up until now, I've led a disgustingly healthy existence—so healthy that I used to think a blood test meant tracking a wounded animal in the woods at night. I'm closing in on fifty-two, and I haven't spent a night in a hospital since Eugenie was born in 1990.

Over the years, I've had a few close calls, though, including a breast cancer scare. It was December 1997, right before Christmas. I was showering on a Sunday evening when I felt a marble-size lump under my right arm. I knew something was wrong. I came out of the bathroom, sat on the bed, and stared out the window. My life screeched to a halt. I broke down in sobs. Was I meant to die? Would this be the last Christmas with my girls?

I made an appointment with my doctor to have a needle biopsy. It would be three days before I'd get the results. Those were the longest three days of my life—three days when the orchestra in my mind blared out of control, the strings and brass in clashing time. Three days of lurking terror.

Then came the call from my doctor. I took a deep breath, fully expecting the worst. Then my doctor told me the news. What had begun as a scary possibility was swiftly understood as something quite minor: a benign cyst.

I cried for joy. My first real understanding of mortality slowly began to move my spirit. I educated myself on breast health, became an advocate for regular screening, and now support a number of breast cancer organizations to raise awareness whenever I can.

Since hitting my fifties, I felt that my body was shifting, and just maybe I was approaching menopause. I am a thousand shades of embarrassment even mentioning the word because I never wanted to admit that I could be. But I know I'm changing, sometimes as fast as day to day. As I get older, there are many things I must adjust to, and yes, simply admit. I am no longer the nubile nymph of my youth. I know what you're probably saying, we're not getting older, we're getting better. Sure, right! I'm much better at walking slow and boy, can I sit through a sunset! But I'm proud to say that at least I can still dance till dawn.

The thought of heading into menopause didn't seem to penetrate my psyche until I started to see and feel some of the signs: dry skin, low energy, and a depression that could not be attributed to life getting in my way. Other strange things had been happening to my body that I couldn't understand. I would wake up in the middle of the night, drenched in sweat and feeling anxious. During the day, I'd get a restless feeling in my gut, which would seem to turn into an intense heat. I'd start sweating profusely and it felt as if my whole body were going to explode. I felt as if I had been stranded in the Sahara Desert every night.

The hot flashes led to less sleep and less rest—both of which affected my fatigue levels. Some days I could barely get out of bed in the morning. That's just not me; usually I bound out of bed with enormous strength and energy. But lately I had been feeling as dead as a body on an embalmer's table.

So then I started thinking, "Oh, no, here comes menopause."

I went to see Robin's doctor, Prudence Hall, MD, at the Hall Center in Santa Monica, California, a Zen-like place with fountains and calming music. It looks more like a spa than a doctor's office. Dr. Hall is a lovely, striking woman. When you meet her, you can't help but keep looking at her. At age sixty, she looks many, many years younger, and that alone made me an instant believer in whatever she had to offer.

Robin was with me when Dr. Hall reviewed the results of my blood tests. Their eyes widened and their jaws dropped. I suppose the only thing worse would have been if I was asked to write my will on the spot.

Dr. Hall proceeded to tell me that the test showed that my hormone levels were far lower than those of normal mortals, and certain hormones were in a race to see which could deplete first. So far, my thyroid hormone was in the lead. It was practically nonexistent.

Optimistically, Dr. Hall informed me, "You're in charge of

your health and you're in charge of your care. You've got to be a partner with me and we'll figure out what's best for you."

With my multiple hormone deficiencies, Dr. Hall suggested a regimen of bioidentical progesterone, estrogen, and testosterone; thyroid replacement; and DHEA pills. Like every woman worldwide, I've been bombarded with news stories on HRT (hormone replacement therapy). Foolishly I thought my decision was a simple one: Do I take hormones or not?

Hormone replacement, I knew, was controversial. So naturally my mind, which always tends to ruminate about what might happen, what could happen, or when it will happen, began to assault me. I started having dark thoughts about weight gain, bloating, and blood clots.

Can it all be trusted to be safe and effective? Do I take testosterone even though I might develop facial hair? How might I attract a man once he sees me with a mustache? How many supplements do I take, and in which order, and will my body know what to do with them?

But Dr. Hall explained to me that bioidentical hormones are safer than synthetic estrogens and progesterones because they're made from plants. (Synthetic hormones are made from horse urine.) This form of medicine is like "inner plastic surgery" because it kind of works from the inside out. I was always one to buy creams that promised to reduce my wrinkles or make my hair resemble what it was like when I was twenty. After all, hope springs eternal. I could make a rhinoceros's hide look as smooth as silk with all the youth serums I've bought. Anyway, Dr. Hall's approach all made sense and I agreed to go on the regimen.

She also helped me fine-tune my diet. I didn't want to go too far in the direction of eating food that's supposed to be good for you, because my Celtic roots crave shepherd's pie and Yorkshire pudding.

We talked about inflammation in the body. Dr. Hall explained that inflammation protects us. It helps our bodies get rid of foreign matter like bacteria and toxins, keeping them from spreading into other tissues and organs. Its protective responses—redness, heat, pain, and swelling—help the body get rid of foreign substances and prepare injured tissues for repair. Occasional inflammation is part of the normal healing process.

But like just about everything, inflammation has its downside. When it's chronic, it becomes destructive. Repeatedly inflamed tissues become damaged and break down, creating diseases.

To reduce inflammation, I had to replace refined sugars with whole grains and fruit, watch the balance of fats in my diet, and cut back on organ-damaging alcohol.

I pledged in my diary the following: *I definitely know I must renounce sugar out of my life. Conclusion: renounce sugar, and believe in the power of doing so, because I want to be healthy, physically and mentally, and I want to see my grandchildren grow up. I've got to get the junk out of my system. It causes inflammation and my body to hurt.*

I was also prescribed vitamin supplements such as a multiple vitamin–mineral pill, iron, vitamin D, and a formulation designed to boost my adrenal glands. The adrenal glands play a part in regulating mood and energy and helping us deal with stress.

These grape-size glands manufacture and secrete potent hormones that are essential to your health and vitality and have profound consequences for the way you think and feel. Without the adrenals' hormones, you would die—which further explains all the weird symptoms I had been experiencing.

I have always believed in nutritional supplements and holistic remedies. My grandmother was a homeopathic doctor, in fact. When I was eighteen years old, she healed me of glandular fever using homeopathic medicines.

Homeopathy is a natural pharmaceutical science based on the premise that "likes are cured by likes," also called the Law of Similars. In other words, homeopathic therapy uses a medicinal substance with a "symptom picture" that is most similar to the symptoms of the person who is sick. For example, sleeping difficulties caused by drinking too much coffee could be treated by taking small amounts of the homeopathic remedy Coffea. Thus, homeopathy works with the body's inherent recovery process.

I have long used homeopathic remedies prescribed by Dr. Peter Procuik, a man so gifted in his field. One of the remedies I tried (reluctantly at first) was Lachesis, made from the venom of the bushmaster snake, which lives in the jungles of Central and South America. This remedy is given for headaches, palpitations, appendicitis, sore throats, and menstrual pains. And it is very effective—at least it was for me. So I believe in homeopathy. When I take homeopathic drops and pills, I feel much calmer and more secure, and I definitely have more clarity.

And now, with Prudence's help, too, I headed off with a shopping bag of creams, potions, and pills—and a feeling of hope.

I get up in the morning, take my thyroid medicine, and spread creams in places I don't think we need to discuss. As one of my daughters says, "Let's not go there." I finish by taking the rest of my supplements.

The regimen has made a huge difference. I feel like a new woman. The huge blanket of fatigue and negativity has been lifted. I feel like I am walking on air and I have not looked back. Sleep comes easily now, and I find that I'm calmer and able to tolerate everyday stresses better than before. Moreover, I've been able to avoid the hot flashes and other uncomfortable symptoms associated with menopause. My energy is back, and my skin glows again.

I'm so pleased with the results that I've encouraged my friends who are in their forties and fifties to get their hormone levels tested. I want every woman in the world to know that they don't have to feel so awful. Just because you're in your fifties doesn't mean you have to turn into an old lady.

Before I left Prudence Hall's tender care, she handed me a little card. Written on it were these words:

The only lasting beauty is the beauty of the heart.—Rumi

NUGGETS:

- Make sure you have your hormones well balanced. When our bodies start losing that juice, we can begin to wither and dry up.
- Talk to your doctor, and consider bioidentical hormones and thyroid help.
- More exercise means less aging—so get active with something you enjoy.
- Don't go overboard with plastic surgery. If you've had too much lifting and tightening, you can start to look as though you just came out of a wind tunnel.
- Healthy aging comes from adopting an attitude that is positive about life.

From: Martha Beck

To: Sarah

Relax. Breathe. Feel your heart's desire for love and kindness, and let it be as it is. Offer it memories of love, the way you'd offer milk to a kitten. Gradually you'll begin radiating acceptance to the whole world, and the whole world will accept you.

xoxo

Martha

24 | *Wedding Bells*

*The good times and the bad times have made me the woman
I am today, and I have nothing to regret about that.*

ON THE DAY that Prince William and Catherine
Middleton became engaged—November 16, 2010—I felt like the air
had been sucked out of me. I wanted to die, I really did. I crouched
in a corner, terrified and alone.

Was I jealous? Was I remembering those glorious, heady days

when the whole world was looking at the luckiest girl alive? Would I do the whole thing over again?

Yes, yes—and yes.

I knew in my heart that Kate was absolutely the luckiest girl in the world, as fairy tales go. She would marry her prince.

Like millions of other people, I got the news via a CNN update. Prince William had popped the question in Kenya some time ago, slipping a sapphire-and-diamond engagement ring onto Kate's finger. In doing so, he linked her not just to the pomp and circumstance of royal history but to one figure in particular: his late mother. Diana was the ring's previous keeper. After nine years of dating and will-they/won't-they speculation, it was a headlong step into the glare of the spotlight.

The announcement coincided with a planned trip to India to attend the wedding of a friend. I was happy for the coincidence because I could shield myself from the endless stream of media reports.

But I could not stop thinking about the engagement. I spent my seven-hour flight to India remembering the last wedding held at Westminster Abbey—mine.

1986

Final preparations for the sovereign display began before dawn, as crack marksmen took up their positions on the rooftops and security men disguised themselves as bewigged footmen. By 10:00 AM the first of the 1,900 guests began taking their seats in the abbey. First Lady Nancy Reagan and Prime Minister Margaret Thatcher were in attendance, along with Opposition Leaders Neil Kinnock, David Owen, and David Steel. So, too, were actor Michael Caine,

TV host David Frost, and singer Elton John, sporting purple glasses and a ponytail.

Just ninety minutes before the ceremony, the Queen conferred the title Duke of York on Prince Andrew. By tradition, this title is reserved for the sovereign's second son and had previously been held by King George VI.

Members of the Royal Family began taking their place next to the high altar: Prince Edward, acting as Andrew's best man, the Queen Mother, Prince Philip, Princess Anne, Prince Charles, Princess Diana, and little Prince William. Next, the country's first family took its place on the high altar, across from my mother, Susan, and my stepfather, Hector.

When Andrew and I were engaged, there were some inside the palace who did not want Hector to attend because he was Argentine, and our countries had fought bitterly over the Falkland Islands. I put my foot down hard at this, the first of many run-ins I would have with the powers behind the throne. My father walked me down the aisle at Westminster Abbey, but in my mind Hector was just as much a part of my family.

A few minutes after eleven, the gates of Clarence House swung open to release a matched pair of bay horses and their special freight, the Glass Coach, so named for the large windows on either side. There were but two passengers: myself and my father, who looked dashing in his own father's dark-green morning coat. The crowd outside loosed into a raucous version of "Here Comes the Bride."

We made our ceremonious way along the Mall to Westminster Abbey. With nearly a million people lining the one-mile route, Dad looked desperately flustered. But I was just cruising. This was fun.

As trumpets sounded and thousands roared, my father and I

stepped out of the coach. It isn't so hard to enjoy mass adoration; the tricky part is understanding that it has nothing to do with you, and it rarely outlives an English summer. But on my wedding day all I knew or cared about was that Fergie was in glorious vogue. And as for Sarah, that ugly, valueless, unglamorous creature? No one had seen or heard from her for some time, which was just as I wanted it.

As we reached the Abbey's West Door, adjustments were made to my dress, made from duchesse satin, the creamiest material in the world. Attached to the dress was a fifteen-foot train. We took our places, heard the first notes of the processional, and started down the aisle.

As I moved down that rich strip of carpet, my hair crowned in gardenias, I blocked out the guests in the Abbey and the half a billion people watching me on television.

I stayed calm right up to when the archbishop of Canterbury, Dr. Robert Runcie, looked at me with his big eyes to lead me through my vows. In that moment the immensity of it all pierced my cloud of cool. Although I had drilled my lines, in particular Andrew's middle names—Albert Christian Edward, which I remember as ACE—I stammered over Christian and repeated it twice.

Much was made of the fact that I opted for traditional marriage vows. Diana had taken the modern route, omitting the bride's pledge of obedience, and people expected me to follow suit—I probably went the other way to be different. It was all a moot point with me; to obey him was merely to hear my own soul.

We plighted our troths and exchanged our rings, and the congregation burst into "God Save the Queen." I had become Princess Andrew and the Duchess of York, as well as the Countess of

Inverness and Baroness of Killyleagh, a place in Northern Ireland where I have ancestral links.

Prince William, age four at the time, probably doesn't remember it, but he was a bit of a show stealer. During the forty-five-minute ceremony, the irrepressible prince played on the cord of his hat, wrapping the string around his nose and chewing it like a licorice stick. Undaunted by baleful stares from his mother and grandmother, the second-in-line to the throne pulled out his miniature ceremonial dagger and began poking holes in the dress of Diana's niece Laura Fellowes, age six. Later, as we got into the Coach, the little prince ran toward the carriage, and the Queen hurried to retrieve him.

Back to the palace . . . up to the balcony for our public appearance. Tens of thousands shouted, "Give us a kiss!" Then, obligingly, we kissed.

I was so deeply attached, so profoundly in love. I didn't realize that in getting my prince I would have to give up so much, not least the man himself.

The plane landed in Delhi, India, with a thump that wrested me from my nostalgic reverie. At the Delhi airport, I discovered that British Airways had forgotten to put my luggage on the plane. The kind person who met me insisted that it would come on the next flight. My next destination was Jodhpur, so I made my way to the Jet Airways check-in desk, just to confirm my ticket. Lucky I did, since traveling in India is much different than it used to be. At every turn, you must produce documentation of your travel schedule and proof that you even exist.

I nested in the airport lounge while awaiting my flight to Jodh-pur. Several cups of tea later, I rang my friend Debbie, who would also be attending the wedding.

"What on earth are you doing going to Jodhpur?" she blurted. "We have all just arrived in Jaipur!"

I had to get to Jaipur, but the next flight was fifteen hours away. I hired a driver to take me there—a six-hour trip by car. He ma-neuvered his way skillfully through Delhi, not an easy task. The streets were teeming with people and animals: women in colorful saris and punjabis (two-piece outfits with a matching scarf); the aroma of Indian spices; bicycle carts piled high with building mate-rials, computer equipment, and people; cows and pigs wandering in the streets; motor scooters, rickshaws, and buses so crowded with people they were hanging out the doors and on top of the bus. I realized that the experience of getting from one place to another—

the congestion, the sheer visual confusion—is the actual India, and I loved it.

I arrived at an inn in Jaipur, thrilled to see my friends Debbie and Lulu. My luggage had not arrived, so Debbie loaned me some floaty garments that would make the Indian heat more bearable.

As ancient customs go, the groom travels to retrieve his beautiful bride—which is why the ceremony began in Jaipur. The festivities started with an arrival party for Shivraj, the groom, followed by the wedding. Some years ago, Shivraj had fallen off his horse and became comatose. Nobody ever believed he would come out of the coma, so this was truly a miracle day.

The wedding was a most spectacular traditional Indian affair. It began with *baraat,* an Indian wedding tradition: Escorted by his family, the groom arrived on a white horse, with an elephant trailing behind, beautifully painted and garnished with flowers. Lotus blossoms were everywhere, symbolizing that God is with us.

The whirligig of an Indian wedding—jewelry-embellished women, the swish of silk, the cloying fragrance of jasmine, tinkling laughter—is something to behold. There were colors of every sort, with the exception of black, which by custom is not allowed.

A Hindu priest performed the service. He tied the bride and groom together with a rope at the moment they were officially wed—a traditional ritual that symbolized their new bond.

Next, the bride and groom returned to Jodhpur with the wedding guests, where the "coming home" festivities would continue. We took the train to Jodhpur, along with the whole wedding party. The doors of the train stayed open as we scooted through the countryside, which was so full of color and spirit. I was able to take photos and I clicked away, recording the intoxicating bustle of life in India.

At the reception, fireworks burst in the night sky, dinner was served out under the stars, and a beautiful dancer performed. People ultimately like to sing and dance at Indian weddings, so the band played on, and we danced into the early-morning hours.

On my day of departure, I took a taxi to the airport. I wanted to get an earlier flight from Jodhpur to Delhi. (I was originally scheduled to fly out on November 28.) Changing flights is impossible to do in India—there is a strict no-change ticket policy—because you need proof or documentation that you are leaving on your specific, intended flight. I did not have the required proof for the earlier flight, nor did I even have a seat, since the earlier flight was booked solid.

Debbie and her husband, Leopold, had flown out earlier by private plane. Leopold had never canceled his ticket on the commercial flight from Jodhpur to Delhi, so Debbie suggested that I take Leopold's seat. At least I would have a seat; however, I would have to convince the security officer that I was a man! Downright impossible, for sure.

I spied a round, cuddly-looking chap (I nicknamed him Mr. Cuddles) who seemed to be busy escorting people in and out of the airport. With his help and a few dollars, I bargained my way in.

Some five hours later, as I was about to board, a female security guard got suspicious and caught on to my ruse. She refused to allow me to use the ticket, claiming, correctly, I was not a man! Mr. Cuddles was nowhere in sight to rescue me.

I surrendered to the reality that I'd be staying in Jodhpur, probably until the twenty-eighth. I accepted defeat, when suddenly out of the corner of my eye I saw Mr. Cuddles and asked him to intervene. He negotiated furiously in some Indian dialect with the female guard. She relented, as long as I produced my booking for the twenty-eighth. I scrambled to retrieve it from my BlackBerry so that I could board the plane. I showed it to her, and she was satisfied.

I catapulted onto the plane in the nick of time. I squished myself into a middle seat between two well-fed Indians and kept silent, filled with gratitude. One hour and ten minutes later, we landed in Delhi.

Tired and bedraggled, I still had to fly on to California for a much-needed session with Dr. Phil. I needed to sort through my feelings on Andrew, our past, and the impending Royal wedding.

Dr. Phil didn't waste any time boring in. "How will this wedding affect or involve you? Will that be a stressful thing or a positive thing for you?"

"It's had a huge effect on me. I feel deeply, deeply sad. I made so many mistakes in my marriage that I'd like to do it over again."

"You'll think back to how you once had that opportunity? Will you be excited for Kate?"

"Oh, completely. It's wonderful for her, and I know how she feels. But the other side of me is looking and cringing, knowing that I blew everything."

Dr. Phil sat for a moment and glowered a bit. "You don't get a do-over, and that stuff will never go away. What you have to do is not react to what happened. Instead, react to what you say to yourself about what happened. If you say, that is the dumbest thing ever in the history of the world, and therefore my life is over, because of bad decisions made, you are sitting on the sidelines waiting to die and feeling sorry for yourself. Then what will your legacy be in this life? Will it be that you made a couple of bad decisions during your marriage? Or will it be what you create from this point forward in your life?"

"But why did I make so many mistakes?"

"It's a matter of intention," he explained. "Were you trying to sabotage your marriage? Were you trying to sabotage your reputation?"

"Not in a million years."

"So the intention was not evil?"

"Correct."

"That has to matter to you."

"Okay."

In typical Dr. Phil fashion, he told me, "Your enthusiasm is underwhelming. This has to matter to you."

"I caused Andrew great pain, and I would never cause anyone great pain intentionally. But I caused him pain. How do I live with that?"

"He has healed, has he not? And he has forgiven you?"

"Yes, completely."

"And he loves you?"

"Yes, completely. But leaving Andrew was the biggest mistake of my life."

"Will you ever reconcile with your ex-husband? Will you ever live together as husband and wife?"

"I don't know. We are a family and we always will be. He is a great, great man. We do have this extraordinary love. And the girls benefit from it."

More Dr. Phil advice tumbled out: "You're always talking about things in your life you have blown. Stop adding to the list. Instead, look at all the opportunities you have created for yourself. You have the responsibility to claim those opportunities. Stop sitting on the sidelines feeling sorry for yourself. Tell yourself, 'I could not be more proud, and mean it from the core of your soul. In Texas we call that cowboying up. So cowboy up, girl. There is life ahead of you."

Dr. Phil gave me plenty to think about, and I did.

It took massive meditation and awareness of my own self-punishment, but I turned my thinking and my emotions into a reservoir of positivity. As I thought about the wedding, I was sure Prince William knew that he was choosing more than a wife: he was choosing a queen, whose duties will be demanding. He is asking not just for her hand, but for her to join him in a life of public service in which every move will be subject to the highest degree of scrutiny by an unrelenting twenty-four-hour media.

The demands of royal protocol and of a celebrity-obsessed culture are challenging at best. The mixture of the two can create psychological stress which, trust me, I know all about.

Although I would not be invited to the wedding, I felt so much pride in knowing that my daughters would shine with beauty and that their handsome father would look magical in his naval uniform. I remarked to him: "That is the very same uniform in which you were married!"

"Not really, Sarah," he reminded me. "I've been promoted since then!"

> *From: Martha Beck*
>
> *To: Sarah*
>
> *Hello, Dear!*
>
> *Lead yourself the way you'd lead a horse—firmly, with decisiveness, but no beating. Beaten horses get depressed. They balk. They kick. This, to me, is clearly the reason the wine releases a part of you that seems out of control. It's the part of you that resists being beaten.*

Think how you feel when the press beats on you. Does that make your life work better? If not, then how could replicating it yourself be effective?

Please notice which experiences and memories take you into peace and relaxation (even when you're very physically and men-

tally active). You're creating the pattern for the rest of your life. You get to stitch it together out of the best experiences you can imagine.

xoxoxoxo

From: Mark Nepo
To: Sarah
Dear Sarah,
Thanks for sharing so much of your journey. We thought of you the other day as we took a nice long walk in the pine forest. I looked to where we sat on that fallen tree and wondered how you are. All the best will continue to unfold.

Much love,
Mark

From: Marina
To: Sarah
Darling Sarah,
You are incredible, and I have never doubted that you would come out of it all and even stronger, my dear friend. Remember, nothing and nobody can ever break our spirit. We have learned so much and are better persons for it. Masses of love to you and your wonderful Beatrice and Eugenie. They are always a tribute to you.

Marina

25 | *Adventure as Therapy*

I want something larger and more lasting than the latest three-column spread.

ONE NIGHT IN December 2010 I lay awake beneath a flapping tent on a frozen lake, trying to stay alive in temperatures that will freeze your flesh in a matter of seconds and wondering if it were possible to feel any more wretched. Under a special black parka—a combination of thick down and a windbreaker—I was wearing long underwear, my heaviest ski pants, a shirt, and two very heavy sweaters. On my feet were caribou-skin mukluks, or Eskimo boots; on my hands, mitts with wool liners.

The wind roared through an open space in the tent, and I was shivering. Then I realized I was going to have to crawl out of the tent and go to the bathroom in a howling, freezing storm. How, I wondered, had I ended up in the frozen Arctic, hunkering down in subzero weather, and praying that I didn't freeze, at least not while my pants were down around my ankles?

Welcome to impossible2Possible (i2P). I2P, in case you've never heard of it, is an outdoor adventure and educational expedition; a bare-bones, no-frills, physical, mental, and emotional challenge. It engages and inspires people of all ages to the i2P philosophy that we're all capable of the extraordinary in our lives. I suspect that most of the people who enroll in i2P do so because they're in a rut or going through a transition. That's why I signed up.

Something deep inside me, though (perhaps the gentle stirrings of the real Sarah?), told me I needed to do this, that I needed a life-and-death challenge to get me closer to the woman I wanted to be, and so I forged ahead into the unknown.

The first challenge was simply choosing the adventure. I met with Ray Zahab, i2P's founder, in Los Angeles. Ray informed me that at the time when many people are fleeing winter's bite by heading south to sandy beaches and fruity umbrella drinks, I'd be heading north. I'd be dropped off on the frozen-solid Great Slave Lake in the Canadian Northwest Territories—a place nearly as big as India. "My friends will think I've gone mad," I thought.

From there, I'd traverse the lake in a twenty-six-mile trek to the town of Yellowknife, a place I knew very well. Andrew and I had our honeymoon there twenty-five years ago. We took a two-week canoe trip with six other hearty souls down the Hanbury River. Andrew had made similar excursions with friends back in his Ontario school days, and he hankered to share with me the joys of white water. Touched by Andrew's eagerness, I'd said yes. The pilot who had flown us into Yellowknife predicted that he would have to pull me back out within forty-eight hours; he even kept his seaplane on standby.

I remember how we'd gratefully stumbled out of the tight, narrow seats where we had been confined for the two-hour flight from Yellowknife. As the silence engulfed us, so did the mosquitoes, voraciously attacking each smidgen of exposed flesh as if they hadn't seen a human for months. In fact, they probably hadn't. We had to wear bug nets—which made eating quite challenging.

Every day we paddled for three hours—which seemed to me like an eternity—and I eased my unused muscles into the rhythm of long strokes. I reveled in the freedom of the wilderness. We chased molting, flightless Canada geese downstream ahead of us.

Eventually we came to some rapids. Sadly the water was too low, so we could not go through on canoes. We portaged with seventy-pound packs on our backs across rocky ground, stone stepping. I didn't envy a mule or donkey, though I certainly looked like one. Once we made camp on a sandy beach that seemed transplanted from Cape Cod.

I remember that on the last day of the trip, we'd nestled into a hotel and sunk into a hot bath. The vacation turned out to be fun and memorable, with the exception of the mosquitoes. Now I wondered if it would be a painful reminder of the mistakes I'd made in life. And that would make this challenge a much more emotional one for me.

Ray is a fortysomething Canadian with rugged good looks and a supremely fit physique. He is one of the most insightful, inspiring people I've ever met. It is hard to believe that he was once a pack-a-day smoker. Ten years ago, realizing he wanted more from life, Ray decided to adopt a healthier lifestyle and get active. He told himself he'd do the very best he could moving forward, and there was no looking back from there.

Ray started reading about ultramarathoning and a race in the Yukon that was one hundred miles nonstop—four times the distance of a marathon. He couldn't believe it. How did runners get past the emotional and physical barriers, he wondered? There was a photo of one guy pulling the sled with all the supplies, looking so happy for his accomplishment, but what struck Ray was that he looked like a normal guy. It was like he was speaking to Ray from the page of the magazine. At that instant, Ray decided then that he had to do this—and became an ultramarathoner himself.

Pushing the envelope even further, Ray and two other ultrarunners made history in 2007 by running 4,300 miles across the entire Sahara Desert, battling blinding sandstorms, biting and stinging insects and other pests, and the many physical afflictions that accompany a run across an entire continent. In the process he learned about the serious, life-threatening lack of clean water in Africa. The run was documented in the film *Running the Sahara*, directed by Oscar winner James Moll and narrated by Matt Damon. One of the goals of the film is to raise awareness of the water crisis in Africa.

Ray has completed eight major expeditions to date and was recently a member of the South Pole Quest and the Siberian Express teams, and in early 2011 he ran the length of the Atacama Desert. In 2008, he founded impossible2Possible based on the principle: The only limitations we face are those we place upon ourselves. If my survival was at stake in the Canadian Northwest, Ray would be my first choice as a companion.

Ray assured me that any person in average physical condition could tackle this adventure, but I had my doubts. I had ignored the fact that I was an out-of-shape fifty-one-year-old, more accustomed to tailored suits and heels than backpacks and parkas. My physical stamina certainly paled beside Ray's. When I found out that I'd be hauling a fifty-pound pack for twenty-six miles and that I was advised to do aerobic and weight-bearing training seven days a week for five weeks in advance, I started to wonder if I had the strength and endurance for this, especially after living in flat London.

Ray assigned a trainer named Aaron Ferguson to work with me and get me fit. An Australian, Aaron is funny, bright, and a wonder—not to mention incredibly cute—and a shining little piece of gold dust. Aaron, whose favorite expression is "Let's crank," specializes in preparing people for extreme adventures. If I was to succeed, I'd need someone with Aaron's expertise.

The first thing we did was head to a flower mart to get a feel for the cold. Ray, Aaron, and I stepped into the cooler. After mere minutes I was intensely aware of how cold I was, so cold, in fact, that I had trouble forcing the muscles of my mouth to form words.

"As cold as it is in here," Ray said, "it's going to be forty times as cold in Yellowknife."

Brrrrrrrr.

Aaron had been to Yellowknife himself. "Ten people died during the two weeks I was there."

Hearing that story did not comfort me. "Really? What, because of the cold?"

"Yes. Frostbite. They didn't have the right gear."

"Nice cheery thought."

The more I heard about this adventure, the more daunting it became. The key for me would be to stay mentally strong. If I didn't, I'd fail, and in this case, failure could mean death.

For the last fifteen years I had exercised—lifting weights and jogging—but Aaron changed my workouts to train for my trip.

One workout was to drag a tire tied behind a backpack. I silently grumbled, "You've got to be kidding."

This exercise simulated the sled-pulling I'd do across the snow-covered frozen lake, although the sled would be heavier. My first impression was, "Oh, my God, I'm so fat!" It was tough and exhausting; it felt like I was pulling the fifteen-foot train of my wedding dress. Then Aaron told me to run with it! The next day my hamstrings were screaming.

More training exercises followed: long daily hikes in the Malibu hills—treks that got longer and harder each day; and running on the beach and up and down sand dunes—all fueled by a vegetable- and carb-rich nutritional program Ray had designed.

One night Aaron and I reached the peak of one of the hills and were entertained by a fiery red sunset over Los Angeles and a chorus of birds singing a nighttime lullaby. I got out my camera and began clicking away.

Aaron and I chatted a lot during these training sessions.

"Actually, I think I've decided that it's time for a boyfriend. That's what I need, Aaron, a boyfriend."

"All right. Let's get running."

"Yes, actually, I've got to get fit in order to attract him."

"It's time to get you a man."

"He has to be fit, humorous, spiritual, kind, and love animals."

I mentioned to Aaron that I had married England's best-looking prince.

"Are you thinking about getting back together?"

"I don't think they'd have me back. But I hope someday there will be somebody lovely who will be with me. I don't know who it's going to be; who knows, it might even be Andrew."

Then suddenly I didn't want to talk about it anymore. The topic threw off my focus.

Another time Aaron and I were training in Britain over Christmas when it was 10 degrees below. The snow was so thick that we couldn't run, so we walked, slip-sliding the entire time. I started talking to him about my wretched mind chatter and my people-pleasing addiction. He told me this amusing story, which is one of Aesop's fables:

Once a man, his boy, and a donkey were traveling to a city that was very far away. On their way there, they passed many villages and met many different kinds of people who believed very different things.

One day, the two travelers and their donkey walked into a village where the people believed that youth was to be honored and revered. When the villagers saw the man and his boy walk into town, they stopped them and said to the man, "You're not taking proper care of the young boy. He should be honored and allowed to ride on the donkey instead of walking." So the man put his boy on the donkey, and they rode out of town.

The next day, they came to a village where the people believed their elders should be respected. When they saw the man walking by with his son riding the donkey, they stopped him and said, "You are the eldest. You should be the one riding the donkey." So the man lifted his son off the donkey and got on it himself.

On the next day, the three came to a village where everyone believed that people are the highest creatures in a world order that has been created by God, and that all other creatures should serve people as their masters. They laughed at the man and boy and said that they should both ride the beast and whip him with a stick if he refused to carry them. So they both got on the donkey and rode him out of town.

Finally, they came to a village in which the people believed that animals have rights just as humans do and that animals should be respected and honored just as much as humans are, if not more. When they saw the man and his boy riding the poor, tired donkey, they became angry with them and said, "The poor donkey has been doing all of the work and you have done none of it. The donkey has just as much right to ride as you do." So they got off the donkey. He and his son cut a strong pole and tied the donkey's feet to it so that they could carry him and give him a rest.

They came to a bridge. The donkey's foot got loose and he kicked the boy, causing him to lose his grip on the pole. They dropped the pole, and the donkey fell into the river.

Aaron wrapped it up by telling me: If you continually listen to the opinions of others, try to do what others believe in, and don't stay in your own space, you can kiss your ass good-bye!

Aaron is such a joy—and so positive. We became very close; he is like a little brother to me.

As for our workouts, I discovered that training for a tangible goal increased my motivation. I was positively inspired to push my limits. In a couple of weeks, I had increased my endurance and stamina—no more huffing and puffing. I don't think my legs have ever been stronger. And I just felt better—and more optimistic that I'd be able to survive the challenge.

"Isn't it great to start a health kick?" Aaron asked.

This was a life kick.

From: Martha Beck
To: Sarah
Hello, darling,
You are not alone, and there is nothing to do. Just breathe and allow yourself to melt. The process of metamorphosis drives itself, without your will.

> *Watch the guilt, and offer your guilt-ridden self love.*
> *Watch the shame, and offer your shamed self love.*
> *Watch your fear, and offer your frightened self love.*
> *Watch your sorrow, and offer your sorrowing self love.*
> *Watch yourself disappear, and offer love to it and the self you have not yet become, who can fly.*

You are never boring, you are always good enough. Nothing can stop your mission, and mission is the one thing that will bring you true joy. Align with God, and you will know that. God is always nearer than near.

Much love,
Martha

26 | *The Great Slave Lake*

Vulnerability is a strength.

*T*HINGS CAN GET very cozy inside a fully loaded prop plane. I was cramped and cranky and fired up to start moving. As I looked out the window, I saw nothing but open stretches of ice, when bang-slap, we landed.

As I stepped off the warm plane, the bone-chilling temperature came as a shock. It hovered around –50 degrees. A thin layer of snow on the ice crackled like bubble wrap under my boots. I inhaled and the hairs in my nose froze. This made London seem almost tropical.

I huddled against Ray and Aaron and shivered. I looked around. "I'm going to die right here," I thought, "cold and frozen for the ages."

Landing in Yellowknife made me nostalgic. I conveyed this sentiment in my diary: *I'm back in Yellowknife again, where I went with Andrew twenty-five years ago. This is all really heartbreaking. It brought back old memories again, and he was no longer there. It's all too much.*

Yellowknife is an icebound, gravel-strewn outpost. Twenty thousand people live there—about half the population of the Northwest Territories. Many of them make their living in the diamond mines. The region is known as the Diamond Capital of North America.

Historically, the first residents of the Yellowknife area were the Dogrib and the Yellowknifes, a band of Chipewyans who moved into the area in the early 1800s and were the city's namesake. After the decline of the Yellowknifes, the land was occupied by the Dogrib and other Chipewyans.

From 1789 to the 1920s, Yellowknife was active in the European fur trade and was the site of a trading post. In 1896, miners on their way to Klondike in the Yukon Territory discovered gold at Yellowknife Bay, but there was no great "gold rush" at the time because the area was difficult to get to. White settlement did not begin until 1934, when more gold deposits were discovered. By this time, the advent of air travel made getting to the area easier, and present-day Yellowknife was born. By the late 1930s, Yellowknife was a boomtown, home to three gold mines.

Gold was the lifeblood of the Yellowknife economy for more than forty years, but the gold claims eventually petered out—the last gold mine was shuttered in 2004—and, in 1991, diamonds were discovered. That set off the largest staking rush in Canada's history.

In 2003, Environment Canada ranked Yellowknife number one in the following categories: coldest winter, coldest spring, coldest year-round, most days at −20 degrees Celsius or less, longest snow-cover season, most high wind-chill days, and most extreme wind chill. Perhaps surprisingly, it also ranked number one in sunniest summer and sunniest spring!

It's no coincidence that Yellowknife is one of the world's best places to see the northern lights. Just north of the sixty-second parallel, Yellowknife sits in the auroral oval, a narrow area that circles the North Pole. The region within this band has the highest occurrence of aurora on the planet.

In the past, some indigenous people believed celestial spirits created the ghostly lights. It's only been one hundred years since scientists even vaguely understood what causes the auroras. They occur when high-speed particles from the sun stream toward the upper atmosphere above Earth's two magnetic poles and collide with oxygen and nitrogen. The resulting electric jolts emit bursts of color, which are magnificent.

Ray began sorting out what would go in our sleds: ice ax, ice screws, shovel for all the snow I'd be shoveling, backup navigation, lots of batteries, fishing line, pee bottle, and dehydrated meals. I was overwhelmed and frightened as he loaded this gear onto our forty-pound sleds. I began to doubt whether I could take on this challenge and survive.

So here I was on the Great Slave Lake in a beautiful part of Canada, so far north that hardly anybody lives there. The frozen lake seemed solid enough, and the ice stretched on forever.

This freshwater sea is named after the Slave or "Slavee" tribe of

Natives who peopled its southern shore (no slavery practiced) and is the fifth largest lake in North America. Yellowknife lies on its northern shore.

It's a forbidding location. In summer, surprising heat is accompanied by hordes of hungry mosquitoes—something I knew about from my honeymoon trip. Winter turns the region into a frozen wilderness of slashing storms and bitter cold.

The next several days were packed with new adventures, and I still don't know if I have synthesized everything I experienced on the trip. One thing I can tell you is that not every moment was wonderful. My legs got very tired, and of course I was chilled to the bone, but I pushed on.

I missed my habitual morning shower and afternoon tea. If you've never gone without mirrors or baths or makeup, you probably don't realize how much time you spend primping. Maybe being without these luxuries would help me appreciate my inner beauty. I could also eat as much as I wanted with no guilt, even if it was high-calorie dehydrated food.

Ray reminded me: "You didn't come here to be comfortable. You came here to be uncomfortable and challenge yourself."

However, most of the expedition was fulfilling—physically, emotionally, and mentally; and at times it was exhilarating, even spiritual. The first night there was a fiery red sky. "You know that old saying: 'Red sky at night, a sailor's delight. Red sky in the morning, sailors take warning'?" Ray said. "The sky makes me wonder if the weather is going to turn against us."

A film crew was there, too, and in a funny way, I found their presence comforting. The sound of their voices in the vast, silent wilderness assured me I was still connected to other people. I had a sense of how marvelously and frighteningly dependent we are on human relationships. One member of the crew, Terry Woolf, seemed inspired by my willingness to make the trek. He told me, "I'd go to war with you, because I know you would get me out." His words touched me and warm tears rolled down my frozen cheeks.

During the day we hiked across the ice, pulling our sleds and gear. I'd look around at the bleak landscape—ice, ice, and more ice, no vistas—and sometimes I felt despondent and scared. After the first moment of terror, I forced myself to look around, to ground myself in the physical details of my surroundings, which were certainly devoid of the distractions of society.

As the expedition progressed, my terror gave way to a feeling of competitiveness. I felt taxed physically yet I wanted to make it successfully back to Yellowknife. I went on this adventure course to force myself to break through personal barriers, as if this, somehow, would transform me or crack the shell I imagined was imprisoning the real me. The ice trek was my opportunity.

Of course, survival was uppermost in my mind, too. I had to use my strength, flexibility, and balance, and stay utterly focused. Ice conditions could change hourly. There might be ten inches of ice in one place, and thirty-six inches in another.

Think about it. How many moments do you have in your life where the next second is all that counts?

"Isn't it a good feeling to realize that you're great at something you've never done before?" Ray asked me one day. "Doesn't it make you wonder how many other things you're really good at that you don't even know about yet?" His words had a huge impact. From that small expression of optimism and hope, I recognized that there is a whole world out there to discover and explore.

As the sky grew dark, we pitched our tents—no easy task. If

you didn't set them up right, they'd get wet, and so would you. Setting up my tent made me realize that I was responsible for my life for the first time.

I propped up pictures of my girls and Andrew, and I burrowed deep into my sleeping bag, put a blanket over my face, and closed my eyes. I kept waking up to the sound of the tent moving. And I realized the wind was kicking up. I was desperate to go to the bathroom, and I had to go. I ventured out—it was freezing cold—and managed to go to the loo. I snuck back into the tent without waking up Ray. I felt like I'd racked up another achievement.

As I tried to go back to sleep, I heard wolves howl in the distance. What if a grizzly destroyed all our gear and food the first night out? I ruminated along those lines for a while, until finally I put the thoughts out of my mind, blithely proceeding on the premise that my training, stubbornness, and, mostly, good luck would see me through.

I felt small and alone and insignificant, and the cold night seemed as if it might swallow me up without a trace. And then, for a brief, unforgettable moment, instead of feeling lost, I felt all my barriers and limitations—my body, my mind, my sense of individuality—dissolve, and I was suddenly part of the great sky and everything present; part of the past and all the people who roamed here before me; part of the animals and landscape; and part of everything that was yet to be. It was a spiritual experience and totally unexpected.

The weather grew heavy and a muffling snow began to fall. When we got up in the morning it was a complete whiteout, and blistering cold. Ray left it up to me as to whether we should wait out the weather or forge ahead.

I didn't think it was a good idea to spend another night in the tent. My sheer Sarah redhead stubbornness prevailed, and we pressed on.

We were walking into the wind, so to prevent the chance of frostbite, we had to wear goggles with a face mask. As we walked, the snow came at us in big waves of white. We couldn't even tell where we were.

Then, as if the finger of God had parted the skies, light from above streamed through the clouds. It was a miracle and a divine message assuring us that we'd be fine.

Ray is a master at reading the conditions and hazards in treacherous terrain. "Up ahead is a pressure ridge."

This couldn't be good. "What on earth is a pressure ridge?" I wanted to know.

"It's a long crack in the ice caused by the thawing and refreezing of ice, and it creates a pocket of water under the ice. If we step on it, we might break through and of course get wet—which for us would be catastrophic right now in these temperatures. So this could be dangerous."

I was terrified. If I took one wrong step, I could fall through the ice into the water and die. No matter what anybody says about ice conditions, it's no fun to find out that you've made a mistake.

Ray skillfully maneuvered us around the pressure ridge and told me exactly where to put my feet. We made it.

My face turned extremely cold. Ray tried to lift my face mask but it had frozen against my nose. He noticed a huge patch of frostbite starting. "Sarah, it doesn't look good, and with frostbite, you don't take any chances."

Frostbite is the poetic name for a serious health issue: frozen skin. The cold wind whipping across my face had caused it. I required medical attention, so Ray called a Dr. Affleck, who rode out on a snowmobile to help me. The frostbite wasn't severe, and he made an adjustment to my face mask that would help it. I wasn't going to let frostbite, fatigue, or anything else stop me from finishing.

At long last, up ahead was Dettah—the "ice road" back. When the mercury plummets to –50 and peaks; when these lakes and rivers are frozen solid; when steel takes on the structural properties of glass and shatters like crystal—this is when navigable ice roads are formed. Currently, there are about 750 miles of ice or winter roads in the Territories. Ice roads are temporary, cross-country routes carved out of tundra, frozen rivers, lakes, and even the ocean to move heavy supplies and equipment into remote areas. Depending on the terrain, specially equipped semitrucks, bulldozers, or loaders driven by ice truckers are used to haul trailers on wheels or sleds. While building, maintaining, and operating on ice roads is difficult, dangerous, and time-consuming, it is cheaper than moving goods by air. And traveling on them is like a journey back to a time before the railroad came, when the one way to move anything of any size, other than by river, was cross-country over rugged trails with a bullwhacker and a team of oxen. The Dettah ice road took us straight into Yellowknife.

I had made it, and no worse for the wear. I threw my hands in the air and shouted, "I dedicate all my achievements to Andrew and the girls. They're the blood in my veins, and I'm the blood in theirs!"

While I achieved my objective—to transverse the Great Slave Lake—I realized there is no end to journeys like these, no fixed point of completion. More important, I still carry with me those transcendent moments on the Great Slave Lake, and I know now not just that I do exist, somewhere beneath all the clutter and clatter of life, but that I am an integral part of the whole grand picture.

And when I want to, I can call up those moments and experience that connection again. It comforts me and puts my life in context.

NUGGETS:

- Make the effort to stretch and grow, to conquer your fear, and you can reach phenomenal heights. When you do, you will surprise yourself. You'll achieve something far greater than you could have imagined.
- Expand your belief about what's possible for you. You have been gifted with strength, courage, and capability that you might not yet have fully tapped.
- Dream big. You are capable of more than you ever dreamed is possible for you.
- Explore something new that feels positive.
- Every now and then, step out of your comfort zone. This will help you live the life you are meant to live.

> From: Martha Beck
> To: Sarah
> I think you've probably burned through a lot of adrenaline, which can make you crash and go into your darkest thought patterns. Remember that "depressed" sounds just like "deep rest." That's what your body and brain are trying to do—deep rest. Lie down whenever you can, and think about all the moments of sweetness in your past. Wrap them around you like a blanket. Rewiring your brain can be that gentle, and right now it must be.
>
> Lots of love,
> M

27 | *Kamalaya*

Serenity is not freedom from the storm,
but peace amid the storm.

*F*ROM THE HARSH subzero conditions of the Arctic, I journeyed to the warmth of Thailand, where I would spend time at Kamalaya Wellness Sanctuary and Holistic Spa on the south coast of Koh Samui, an island in the Gulf of Thailand. Koh Samui, also known as "the island of the coconuts," is the third-largest Thai island. Before the 1970s, when backpackers discovered Koh Samui, it was a tranquil home mainly to coconut farmers and fishermen. Buddhist monks have long favored Koh Samui as a sanctuary for spiritual retreat. The island, they say, has a special energy that enriches and enlightens their spiritual path and helps them connect more profoundly with the universal energies.

Kamalaya's facilities and accommodations encircle a centuries-old cave, once used by Buddhist monks as a place for meditation and spiritual retreat. The tradition of these monks continues at Kamalaya and adds an aura of spiritual and sacred energy to the physical beauty of the land.

The Monks' Cave is always open, and guests are welcome to enter this sacred space for quiet contemplation and meditation. For everyone at Kamalaya, the cave provides spiritual nourishment and a peaceful break to lighten and brighten the day.

What lured me to this magical place was Dr. Prudence Hall's recommendation that I take some time out for meditation and inner work. I signed up for a ten-day retreat. My sister Jane went along.

Kamalaya's promotional literature promises solutions for detox, stress and burnout, fitness, and weight control. The spa's team of international naturopaths can personalize health programs from an extensive range of holistic medicine, spa, and healing therapies.

No one checked our baggage for M&M's and other contraband, but once we registered, it was good-bye to processed food of any kind until the day we left. Nor could we sneak off to the nearest Thai food restaurant. I was envious that Jane was there to tough out the spa's detoxification program, whereas I was there to eat (healthily) and rest.

I protested that I wanted to go on detox, too. I was informed that detox was out of the question because I had exhausted my body and it would be unable to cope with such a stringent regimen. I wasn't allowed to do much exercise either. All I was supposed to do was rest, sleep, and eat a bit of protein each day. Any weight I lost would not be due to a low-calorie diet, but to balancing myself through rest, nutrition, and the proper treatments. I stopped arguing and relented.

Jane would enjoy meals that were far more appetizing than what you would expect to encounter in a detox program. A four-course à la carte detox dinner, for example, featured baby spinach and arugula salad with pumpkin seeds and watermelon vinaigrette, clear hot-and-sour mushroom soup, zucchini spaghetti with curried pumpkin sauce and cauliflower rosettes, and fresh papaya with lime. She drank various detox beverages. They were made from ingredients believed to cleanse the liver: pineapple, strawberries, vegetables, herbs, and wheatgrass—all of which are said to cleanse the liver and kidneys.

I looked over the spa menu, and I started to sweat. There were more options than I could count. Did I want to relieve tension . . . open up the energy channels of my body . . . balance my emotions . . . or unveil my true self? I wasn't sure. Would I want to be calm but also energized? Or perhaps I needed to be energized and balanced? Should I train hard in the gym, swim, or run along a beach? What about just lying in the sun? Or have manicures and pedicures? I settled on massage therapy for calm and acupuncture for energy and balance.

My massage therapist was a pretty Indian lady called Asha, and she knew exactly how to relieve tension in my body. Some people are perfectly quiet during massage sessions, but I am a talker.

"Do you have children?" I inquired.

"I have a little girl named Amala."

"Where is she?"

"She is home in India."

"How often do you get to see her?"

"Only about one month a year."

I immediately thought of my friend Salli, who always looks so sad. I asked her one day, "Why are you so sad?"

"I want to be home with my children, but I can't give up work to be a full-time mum."

Out of the blue I wrote a note to Salli and told her about Asha and Amala. I wrote, "Salli, please be grateful that you have your children with you every day." There are lessons everywhere in life, and I just wanted Salli to put things in perspective, because the experience of motherhood can vary so greatly from woman to woman.

My acupuncturist was a kind, loving Chinese gentleman named Andre. As we chatted, I learned that he and his wife, Gon, were about to become parents.

I've had acupuncture before, which means I've spent some time lying around like a fleshy pink pincushion. Andre inserted needles painlessly into my skin to stimulate my liver and kidney functions and to detoxify and strengthen my blood.

Andre also did a technique called moxibustion. It is a traditional Chinese medicine technique that involves the burning of mugwort (moxa), a small, spongy herb, to facilitate healing. The purpose of moxibustion, as with most forms of traditional Chinese medicine,

is to strengthen the blood and stimulate the flow of qi (energy).
Andre's therapies calmed me down, healed me, and motivated me
to come back for more.

Another friend was Khun Pla, a Thai native with a megawatt
smile. He came to see me every day and escort me to breakfast,
where I sat at a table overlooking the sea, at eye level with swaying
palm trees and birds flying about, and I felt as though I were sitting
in a tree house. I sipped a special brain tonic smoothie and watched
two male lizards trying to attract a female. Their courting rituals
were wonderfully bizarre. Whichever lizard could inflate his throat
the furthest was the winner. Well, there was a clear winner. His
wings appeared, and he flew off with his new lady love.

Khun Pla said he would be back. I said, *"Khob khun ka"* (which

means "thank you" in Thai), and he put his hand together and said the same. Khun Pla was full of *jaidee*, meaning kindness.

Later on in the day, I'd sit on the terrace, sip a protein drink, and watch nature bustle by like on Fifth Avenue the day before Thanksgiving. Nature really is its own Disneyland, and I stand and stare as described in the poem "Leisure" by William Davies:

> *What is this life if, full of care,*
> *We have no time to stand and stare.*
> *No time to stand beneath the boughs*
> *And stare as long as sheep or cows.*
> *No time to see, when woods we pass,*
> *Where squirrels hide their nuts in grass.*
> *No time to see, in broad daylight,*
> *Streams full of stars, like skies at night.*
> *No time to turn at Beauty's glance,*
> *And watch her feet, how they can dance.*
> *No time to wait till her mouth can*
> *Enrich that smile her eyes began.*
> *A poor life this is if, full of care,*
> *We have no time to stand and stare.*

The emphasis at Kamalaya is not only on physical health but also on emotional and spiritual well-being. There are shrines dotting the entrance, and prayer flags are strung between the trees. A candlelit statue of Buddha graces the reception area where you are greeted by the sound of running water and ponds full of lotus flowers. The atmosphere was so peaceful, it was as if the world could begin and end there. What wonderful, spiritual escapism. This spiritual isolation is part of Kamalaya's mystique.

Kamalaya is a cluster of different types of buildings, from hillside suites to beachfront villas, all sitting on a hilltop with spectacular views of the beach, sea, outlying islands, and the lush jungle of palm trees, leafy ferns, and every type of tropical foliage imaginable.

The windows in our room were enormous and the views of the landscape were heart-melting, perched as we were on a hilltop looking across to the long stretch of beach. The terrain was graced by blossoms of a thousand vibrant colors—bougainvillea, hibiscus, and lotus flowers floating delicately on ponds, lovingly placed everywhere by Mother Nature herself. All around me I could hear the cacophony of nature: humming crickets, serenading frogs and lizards and enough chirping songbirds for a chorus. This outdoor playground filled an empty space inside me, the spot that always longs for a connection to nature. Filled with a sense of wonder, appreciation, and humility, I felt a world away from the usual chaotic start to my day—meetings, email, and the other hurdles of life.

Kamalaya was founded by John and Karina Stewart. Karina is a fit, serene brunette and a doctor of traditional Chinese medicine. She has designed and directed medical detoxification programs and conducted "Awakening" retreats in several cities. Her training and study of Asian healing traditions are evident in Kamalaya's integral wellness approach, which aims to access the inner healing power within each person.

John is a tall, handsome, strongly built man in his fifties from Canada. He spent sixteen years devoted to a life of service and spiritual studies in a Himalayan community. He embraced a traditional yogi lifestyle and developed qualities of patience and discipline. John is one of the calmest, most holy people I have ever come across.

Recovering from a bout of ill health in 2000, John was drawn by the healing nature of Koh Samui. He stayed four months to rest and regain his health with the help of local herbs and his, by then, wife Karina. Between them they conceived the idea of a wellness sanctuary combining his spirituality and her interest in health and diet. Both fell under the island's spell—and, in 2003, a spa was born.

For seven years, John was a devout teacher of the works of Haidakhan Babaji, a round-faced, black-haired holy man from the Himalayas who died—or, as his followers say, "left body"—in 1984. Babaji's spirit, however, lives on as a masculine manifestation of Shiva, who, with Vishnu and Brahma, form the supreme Hindu trinity.

Although Babaji appeared in India as a Hindu because that was the religion of the people, he didn't come to espouse any particular religion but to show and teach a way of life. He urged the people to "follow the religion that is in your heart." He taught that "every religion leads to the same divine goal."

I was attracted to these teachings because they are not of a fundamentalist nature. Our spiritual path can be anything. We can go back to our own prophet's original teachings and be a better follower, or even if we're not religious, we can be better human beings by cultivating loving-kindness and compassion. It's the intention in our hearts that matters.

Babaji also said he had come to revive the Sanatan Dharma, or the eternal religion of humanity, and to teach three basic principles: truth, simplicity, and love. He emphasized constant repetition of the ancient Sanskrit mantra *Om namah Shivaya*, which roughly translates to "Lord, thy will be done," and to live in harmony. He taught that all material objects were transient and all emotions fleeting. Happiness, Babaji preached, comes about only when a person rises above attachment. That's the only state in which one can truly serve others and find contentment and salvation in this life.

John continued his spiritual searchings under a nine-year tutelage with an Indian saint, Muniraji, who was staying at Kamalaya while I was there. Muniraji was chosen by Babaji to be the leader of the worldwide Haidakhandi community. Wearing a white cotton *dhoti kurta,* he was a tall, slender man with the constant meditative quality that only a saint could have. He looks like an idol, something not quite from this material world. When I met him, I was instantly drawn to him. There is such a powerful feeling of love in his presence. His eyes exude it. It just poured out.

Muniraji teaches Vedantic principles. Vedanta is one of the six main schools of philosophy in Hinduism. In the Vedantic view, our goal in life is to realize, through direct personal experience, the divine nature within our own self. We are never actually lost (which was very good news to me). At worst, we are living in ignorance of our true nature.

I spent a few hours with Muniraji picking up wise words and reflecting on them. One of the first lessons Muniraji taught me is that we are what we project.

"Think of this like an echo: what we shout out comes back to us. If we put out positive thoughts, positivity comes back to us.

"Each of us has a way that we have learned to project to the world. We have practiced it so much that it has become almost invisible to ourselves. Then we wonder why certain things happen in our life and usually end up blaming life, the other person, or the circumstance. That way of thinking makes us victims."

Muniraji's teaching is all about shifting that stance from being a victim in your own life to being accountable for your own life. It's about waking up to see what you are doing and instantly shifting to see that you are powerful, not powerless.

"What do you do about negative emotions?" I asked. His answer: "Let them go," and his subsequent elaboration of this approach to difficulties in life had for me the force of a depth charge, not so much because of the idea—it sounded simple enough—but because of the spiritual authority and power I felt behind it.

Muniraji agreed to do a "fire ceremony" with us one Saturday morning. Fire in the Hindu religion represents both positive and negative. The ritual includes placing sacred offerings to a god or goddess in the fires, so they will, in return, send good things your way. Through mantras, the fire is asked to take the prayers and consumed offerings to the intended Divinity. For example, if one wanted to increase luck and general prosperity, the offerings would be directed to Ganesh, the elephant-headed god of wisdom and success.

We sat cross-legged on mats around the fire, with everyone chanting *"Ohm."* Muniraji began to burn the symbolic offerings: a coconut, more firewood, and then a saffron-dusted potato. This ritual symbolized burning all negatives.

The wind abruptly changed, and all the smoke blew in my eyes. I took it as a sign from the universe that I should close my eyes and stay focused during this solemn ritual.

Afterward, I pressed him for more. "What really is your message?"

"My message is that we all come from one cell—this is scientifically proven—and therefore we are all connected to the Divine. No matter what religion, race, creed, color, denomination—any of what divides us—we are all one."

The next day, I met with Muniraji privately.

"Do you realize you have a very important mission?"

I sat and looked at him and didn't say a word.

"You have the voice of the world."

Privately, I was thinking, "Yes, I have a voice . . . I can talk the hind leg off of a donkey."

I turned serious. "Yes. I want to be the voice of the silent whisperers, the children who have been abandoned without hope."

I was happy at Kamalaya. The experience awakened a place within me that had long been sleeping. Suddenly, I began seeing all the ordinary things of the world in a new light.

From: Seema

To: Sarah

I can't tell you that I know what you are feeling right now—so I won't. All I'll say is this:

You have a pure glow and spirit. I noticed it right away. You have a gift for making everyone around you feel special. My grandfather, whom I loved blindly, once told me that the great man is the one who makes a king feel like a man and a pauper feel like a king. That is you, my dearest friend. You have that gift of making everyone feel special.

S

28 | *Mr. Carpenter*

Once I've achieved something, I am not one to dwell on it. I am ready to move on.

D URING MY SOJOURN in Thailand, I had an unin-
vited guest burrowing outside my room. This didn't really surprise
me since Kamalaya is surrounded by lush forests with all sorts of

wonderful creatures living within them. My visitor wasn't of the human kind; it was a mouse. Like all mice, he was active mostly at night. That's when mice eat, gather food, and do all the things mice do.

This mouse came to knock on my wall every morning at around four o'clock, when it was still dark. He would make the slightest sounds, a little tap-tap here, or a little critch-critch there.

My imagination began to run away with me. In my mind I saw this mouse as part of a loving family, living an interesting life in the jungle, and beyond. I imagined he was building a house for his family outside the walls of my room. I'm sure the mouse thought it was the perfect place, warm and protected—the nicest house he'd ever had. This mouse, I named Mr. Carpenter.

As I lay wide awake, my ear tuned to his work, I'd wonder what kind of house it would be? Maybe a country cottage surrounded by blue hydrangeas . . . a mansion as gorgeous as a movie star's . . . a mighty castle with a large moat to keep out cats . . . or perhaps his own personal high-rise?

After his house was finished, I was sure he'd invite other jungle creatures over for tea. Everyone would bring something good to eat. Miss Squirrel would bring a basket overflowing with nuts and berries. Mr. Rabbit would surprise everyone with crunchy orange carrots. Little Chipmunk would arrive with a bag of tasty acorns. Mrs. Carpenter would have violets on the table and fresh water from a stream to brew the tea. It would be a special party, indeed. And let's not forget Mr. Lizard and his lady love and his cloak of color.

Lots of people view mice as disgusting little creatures and say "Eek" when they see one. There's really no reason to squeal. Mice are fuzzy and warm little balls of fun. They have big ears, inquiring eyes, and the cutest little noses you've ever seen. They also help save lives, because many medical research departments use mice to help find cures for diseases. I never saw Mr. Carpenter, but I envisioned him to be a very handsome little brown mouse.

There was only one problem: Mr. Carpenter was making a little too much noise.

After a while Mr. Carpenter got to be quite irritating—and extraordinarily loud. Early one morning, as he hammered away, I turned on the light and thumped on my bedroom wall.

"Do you please mind going away?" I asked. "I'd like to get some sleep."

Mr. Carpenter became quiet as a mouse for a while. All was going well until he got out his drill and brought in friends to work on his house. They all just showed up, made themselves at home, and helped themselves to Mr. Carpenter's tools. Some mice put up the walls, others worked on the roof, and a few installed the floors. At first I didn't mind that I had extra visitors, but they started making such a racket that I had to speak up again.

"Mr. Carpenter, this is not funny. I need some extra sleep because I am very tired. Can you please stop building your house?"

For one hour I pleaded with him to stop. He liked to work in the dark, so I kept the light on, hoping the illumination would deter him. Mr. Carpenter and his friends finally got bored and stopped. With the light still on, I put on my eye mask and dozed off.

The following day, I approached my friend Khun Pla. I calmly asked him to do something about Mr. Carpenter.

"Mice do not freak me out," I said, "but Mr. Carpenter is noisy. Please return him to the jungle that is the backyard of my room. But don't hurt him, because I would be very upset."

Khun Pla poked around to investigate. He peeked into small

spaces to find signs of Mr. Carpenter. He looked under logs and rocks and in dense shrubs and holes in trees. He finally found the place where Mr. Carpenter lived while building his house—a little ball-shaped nest of twigs and grass among a jungle of weeds. Then he found himself gazing unflinchingly into the eyes of Mr. Carpenter, hiding behind a weed. The mouse moved, finally, showing that it was not a toy.

Khun Pla placed a net over the construction site outside my room so that Mr. Carpenter could not get into the wall. I'm sure Mr. Carpenter watched from the weeds, thinking, "Oh, no. Someone lives there, too, and they know I was there. I'll have to move."

I guessed that he packed up his tools, scurried off to find another place to build his house, and started over.

Khun Pla assured me that Mr. Carpenter was not a house mouse. "He is a field mouse."

I hoped Mr. Carpenter wasn't sad, disillusioned, or frustrated. I yearned to tell him this: Sometimes, like it or not, you're simply better off starting over.

> *From: Suki*
> *To: Sarah*
> *Dear Sarah,*
>
> *I am sending you my prayers and thoughts for your well-being and trust in the Lord that he is giving you much strength and love. You may be feeling that you are passing one of the hardest times of your life at this time, so remember all that you have achieved, which is unique and wonderful.*
>
> *Only a handful of people are chosen by the Lord to actually do good. Are you one of them? Just look at the many sages that have undergone ridicule. Christ was one of them. Be assured that God in what-*

ever form you believe in is there for you, guiding and wiping those tears. But remember you also have a mission that you must not let go of.

Suki

P.S. On Thursday evening at 9 PM I shall be doing a special prayer for you. It is a sequence of special prayers that will take an hour to finish. The prayers are done to change one's luck and fortune. Also, I saw this morning a lovely prayer that Sai Baba wrote which I wanted to share with you:

Will you, my Lord, let go the hold?
You will not, you will not,
You will not let go,
However bad I be.
Will you my Lord, let me waste my years?
You will not, you will not,
You will not let me waste,
However dull I be.
Will you my Lord, let me run to ruin? You will not,
You will not, you will not let me run,
However wayward I be.
Will you Lord let me escape Your eye?
You will not, you will not,
You will not let me escape,
However wanton I be.
You cannot but rush to rescue Your own.
You cannot delay for weighing pro and con;
You cannot stay unconcerned when we weep;
You cannot but respond to the prayers of the poor.

281

29 | *The Ant and the Buzzing Bee*

Life is like a busy train platform at the station. Stop and pop into the waiting room, have a cup of tea. It will still be just as busy when you come out. That is what meditation is. We stop, become aware of the mind, then carry on with our day.

WHILE JANE WAS busy charting her intake of wheatgrass drinks and counting out her vitamin capsules, I was scheduled to participate in meditation sessions. Meditation is not some New Age practice reserved for monks sitting atop mountains.

On the contrary, meditation is an age-old technique that was developed by some of the world's wisest people to help you become silent and truly examine yourself. Studies show that people who meditate feel better and live longer.

There's nothing mystical or magical about meditation, either. If you've ever sat quietly under a beautiful night sky, gazed up peacefully at the moon or stood on top of a hill, looking out at the vista, and felt calm and good, you were meditating. We all do it "accidentally" now and then, but what happens when we do it purposefully? What happens when you really want to meditate?

I was about to find out. But like many of us, I was afraid to meditate because I didn't know how. Do I sit or can I lie down? Do I have to stand on my head with my legs wrapped around my arms to become a more peacefully centered person? Do I chant or stay silent? I can hardly sit still for five seconds, let alone sit in a dark room for twenty minutes. How on earth could I meditate?

I arranged for a private session with Rajesh, an Indian guru with a smile so wide it split his face in two. He had a real spiritual presence, and I hoped he would teach me how to purposefully meditate. Strolling down the main walkway of the spa, I prepared myself, hopefully, for a bit of personal rejuvenation.

For starters, Rajesh wanted me to let go of my crazy mind chatter. He had a rather amusing but enlightened way of showing me how to do this.

"What are some of your bad thoughts, Sarah?"

"Oh, thoughts like I'm worthless, I've failed, I'm fat and ugly—that sort of negative mind chatter."

Rajesh smiled broadly. "Those are poop balloons!"

"Poop balloons?" I admit I found the expression to be an odd turn of phrase.

"Yes, start visualizing those thoughts as balloons filled with poop. See them floating over your head. If you hold on to them, you'll puncture them with your fingernails, and get covered with poop. Let them go; watch them soar out of your sight. Out of sight, out of mind."

I loved the analogy. Negativity is all about poop balloons, not bursting them, but letting them float out of sight. Rajesh's visualization releases any negativity you might be harboring and puts you in a different state of mind.

Next, it was on to meditating. Rajesh instructed me to sit with my legs folded, spine settled but erect, my chest open (rather than slouching), and my hands cupped upward and resting on my knees. At first, I found it difficult to sit quietly. I squirmed and daydreamed. I chewed over past troubles and worried about future ventures. I noticed everything from a mosquito landing on my leg to the squeaks Rajesh made when he walked about in his rain-soaked sandals.

After a few minutes, Rajesh gently encouraged me to let all the noises and distractions fall into the space of the meditation—to not fight them, but accept them. He used the analogy of an ant on your leg. In meditation, you know that an ant is crawling up your leg but you allow it. The same goes for noises or thoughts. You simply listen to them—they don't make any impact on you. They come and go, and you remain just a witness. Meditation is possible in the midst of distraction.

I did as he instructed. I was amazed by the suddenness with which my thoughts stopped and my experience shifted as I sat listening to the sounds around me. By simply allowing, I not only experienced sounds and sensations, but I felt an almost immediate sense of belonging, of being part of the very fiber of life itself.

"Now, inhale through your nostrils. Then, exhale and make a sound like a buzzing bee," he said. "Be aware of the feel of the vibration in your throat, mouth, cheeks, and lips. Hear the sound from within. Repeat this inhalation and exhalation pattern."

I did as he said.

"Feel the resonation of the buzzing within your body," he said. "This connects you to your heart chakra."

The heart chakra is one of many centers of spiritual power in the body. The chakras (a Sanskrit term for "wheel") receive, assimilate, and transmit life force energy. When they're not functioning properly—when they're over- or underactive—the chakras present "blockages" to that energy flow, which cause imbalances in our health and in our lives.

But when the chakras are open and functioning optimally, they allow energy to flow unimpeded from the base of the spine to the tip of the head in an expression of the boundless power of life.

The heart chakra is about love, compassion, and kindness. When it is blocked, we criticize and judge ourselves and cut ourselves off from a loving relationship with ourselves, other people, and the divine. On the other hand, when the heart chakra is open, we can be generous and compassionate (without giving too much or too little), and we show unconditional love for ourselves and others.

Rajesh believed that I had to unblock my heart chakra, uncover scarred emotions linked to my past experiences and troubled childhood, and reconnect with the little, suppressed Sarah.

"Anything suppressed is like garbage. After a certain period of time, it goes bad. Only by opening up your heart chakra can there be healing and a harmonious flow of energy."

John Stewart joined us to help unblock me.

But I did not want to let them. I put up resistance. I wasn't sure

I wanted to go within and look inside. I was afraid I'd find too much that I didn't want to deal with. I still wanted to live in denial about all the issues in my life and, by avoiding them, I hoped they'd go away.

The two of them sat with me, praying and meditating. After three hours, I lay on a bed to continue meditating. All of a sudden, it felt as if someone were sitting on my chest and suffocating me. These scary sensations lasted for twenty minutes. I thought I was having a heart attack.

Rajesh sat next to me, holding my head in his hands. I began to feel disembodied, as if I were in a trance. I was in a very deep meditation.

Their prayers were so powerful that I felt as if a huge dam in my soul had burst and I began to sob. Almost immediately I sensed a shift. All of this sustained meditation had begun to dissolve my usual ways of coping: constant ruminating, regretting, and rationalizing. It was the most intense feeling I had ever had. Some lifelong barriers like guilt, regret, and self-hatred were coming down. I felt negative energies being released and my heart opening to self-love. I felt connected to the divine through my heart. I realized, for the first time in years that God loves me and that no matter what I've done, God has forgiven me.

Jane and I left Kamalaya in excellent spirits. She was several pounds lighter. My weight was the same, but life felt less heavy — less of a burden — and I felt connected with my spiritual side and the divine within me.

NUGGETS:

- Meditate. Practice clearing the mind and observing passing thoughts as if they were clouds.
- Try the ant and buzzing bee techniques when you meditate. Both are wonderful examples of meditating and you can do them anywhere. Don't be frightened of meditation; it may take only a few minutes a day. It is about listening to your breath and stopping that mind chatter.
- Practice before bed for fifteen minutes, and be in total gratitude.
- Meditation practice is like any muscle—it develops over time, with slow, regular work. If you're impulsive to grab on to its benefits, you'll build a weak foundation of meditation practice. But with sincere, mindful progress, you'll become more patient in your relationships, more serene at the office, and happier when alone. The only thing stepping in your way is you—so get out of your own way and make the necessary changes.
- Remember that you are perfect and whole, just as you are today. Everything you need to be happy and healthy is within you.

> *From: Jeannemarie*
> *To: Sarah*
> *Abundance is now where you are going and where you will stay. You deserve it. God gives it to you and has no intention of taking it away. Let God do the guiding as we hand over our power.*
> *God allows the experiences in life in order to free us from the wrong attachments, and then brings us to Himself.*

30 | *Breakthrough*

The clouds pass but the sky stays.

$\mathscr{B}$Y MARCH 2011, the British tabloids had been working feverishly to vilify Andrew. The tragic thing about being bullied by the media is that it can keep getting horribly worse.

My skin is rubbed thinnest where Andrew is concerned. The reasons are that he has always supported me, and there is absolutely nothing I would not do for him. It was all so unfair. Andrew is a man who does not know how to tell an untruth or behave dishonorably.

A dear friend wrote me the following:

You should boycott the press completely. Go on a tabloid diet for 30 days. Then extend it to 60 and so on. Stop feeding yourself TRASH. And tell everyone around you: "Don't bring me any news that isn't going to directly and positively impact my life." Set that boundary. Be able to say: "This doesn't work for me." And choose what does—that is the mastery of boundaries. Nothing can hurt you unless you give it the power to do so. The lesson you're still learning is that what the newspapers say about you isn't YOU. Not one person writing about you or your family has spent an instant of time trying to know you. They don't know of your hurts, heart's desires, or joys or sorrows. All the things that make up you. You must think of their motivation and intention: to sell newspapers. It's the only thing they think about when they sit down at their computers.

She was right. I now had to be more disciplined than ever.

I was in Puerto Rico visiting a children's cancer hospital when the media lashing began. The bullying would grate in my ears all day—it would grind me down until I found relief in sleep. But there in the dark, the real horror started. Every night I berated myself mercilessly for having caused Andrew's predicament: I did everything wrong; I was to blame. Had he not married me, Andrew wouldn't be so tarnished. I felt intense guilt, and I wanted desperately to fight for him.

When I plummet into dark, abusive thoughts like those, my friend and spiritual counselor Anamika points out that I am in the "triangle."

The triangle has three roles: Victim, Rescuer, and Persecutor. These roles form a cycle of blame and guilt that allows us to avoid taking responsibility for our own emotions, beliefs, or behavior. Just about everyone knows how to assume these three roles, and most of us have a favorite one. We learn how to play the roles in early childhood and we play them thousands of times throughout our lives. Here are brief descriptions of the roles.

- Victim. People often step into the victim role because they are feeling stressed or have low self-esteem or because another person has been persecuting them. The message delivered is "I'm not okay." The victim feels oppressed, helpless, hopeless, powerless, and ashamed. The victim is on the defensive, always trying to survive. Victims get their needs met when they get enough attention.

  Victimhood can have a huge impact on our well-being and some victims identify so much with their role that they even develop physical illnesses to get, and keep, the attention they need. Staying in the victim position keeps us from making decisions, solving problems, and understanding ourselves.

  Whether we know it, or not, most of us react to life as victims. Whenever we refuse to take responsibility for ourselves, we are unconsciously choosing to react as a victim. Inevitably, this creates feelings of anger, fear, guilt, or inadequacy and leaves us feeling betrayed or taken advantage of by others.

- Rescuer. Sometimes people become rescuers because they won't say no and reluctantly take on the responsibility of trying to solve someone else's problem to please them. The rescuer may rescue when he or she doesn't really want to. Yet rescuers feel guilty if they don't rescue. Rescuers love to help, even when they are not asked to do so; helping others is what makes them happy. I asked Anamika, "Well, what is wrong with being a rescuer? What is wrong with saving the world? Isn't this really a good thing?"

"It doesn't mean you can't do nice things for people, as long as you are motivated to act out of pure compassion. Compassion comes from the heart. It has a different energy than rescuing," she explained. "Rescuing winds up being self-sacrificing in every case. We use our own personal energy at our own expense. We sacrifice ourselves and become martyrs. There is never any sacrifice or martyrdom involved in true compassion."

- Persecutor. Persecutors are easy to sum up: They blame, criticize, and shout: "It's all your fault!"

We not only act out these triangular distortions in our everyday relations with others—like trying to rescue someone, feeling like a victim, or punishing another person, but we also play out the triangle internally. We zip around the triangle as rapidly inside our own minds as we do out in the world. We ensnare ourselves on the triangle with dishonest and dysfunctional internal dialogue.

For example, as a persecutor, I came down hard on myself for triggering Andrew's problems, which made me spiral into feelings of self-worthlessness. Inwardly, I cowered to this persecutory voice, fearing it might be right. Then I felt victimized by my own thoughts: "What is wrong with me?" "Why am I so terrible?" "Why do people hate me so much and punish me so much?"

To transcend the triangle, we must recognize that we're in it, or else we can't get out. Which is what I did. There I was in the middle of my triangle—Persecutor, Victim, and Rescuer—all at once.

Andrew called me in Puerto Rico to talk about the problems with the recent press. Immediately I felt like rescuing him, but I pulled myself back. All of a sudden the rescuer role did not feel comfortable to me. Yes, I would be strong for him and I'd be there for him—but this was his problem—and I couldn't be his rescuer or persecute or victimize myself. What I realized is: Other people's problems are not your problems unless you foolishly choose to make them so.

I understood this revelation for what it was: a huge sign that I was healing. I had come to the turning point in my life after finally grappling with who I am. For so long I had been stuck in the triangle, running frantically from one point to another until I had simply worn myself down.

I felt like I had found a new path—a slower, broader road. I would not turn back. I felt stronger, better able to make good choices, treat everything with reverence, assume responsibility for my problems and deal with them, and accept my imperfections. I began to see that I am stronger than anything that could bring me down. At least, I hoped so.

From: Martha Beck

To: Sarah

Hey dear girl!

There's something in our minds psychologists call the "generalized other." It's our fantasy of "everybody," and we believe it's real down to our last breaths. Actually, we often have few genuine representatives of what we think "everybody" is.

It sounds to me (I could be wrong) as though you're focused pretty tenaciously on thinking about your generalized other, which had bad and awful things to say about you. The more you give something your attention, the more it grows. What you know for sure, from the very lips of real people, is that there are many, many individuals who love and support you, no matter what. You notice that, hear it briefly, but go back to obsessing about the negative generalized other, like a person with a hand-washing compulsion who hears the doctor say, "You don't need to fear germs," and feels better for 5 seconds, then goes back to the obsessive fear and the compulsive hand washing all over again.

Your energy is strong—that's why you sell newspapers—and as you turn toward the good, wonderful things will happen. You're making that change already. All is well—and getting better!

xoxo
Martha

13th April 2011
My Dearest Darling Mummy
I have had one of the most incredible journeys this past two weeks and it is all down to you, the best mumsy . . . You have shared your friends, so that me and Jack can have a magical time and created moments that are unforgettable for me. I really can't explain how grateful I am that you are who you are . . . your laugh is the best laugh in the world, and this week we really have laughed. I am just so lucky that I have you to make my world go round because without you nothing is possible . . . you are the most generous mumsy, and I thank you

from the bottom of my soul and the moon and back for everything you give me every day! I am going to miss our special time together, but before we know it we will be back creating more magic ... I love you with all my heart.

Eugeniexxxxxx

31 | *Hugging Pain*

The day goes on.

THERE WAS ONE stop on my journey that I had not yet made. I had never looked into the darkness of a lost part of my life—not full on, without flinching. Until now.

Perhaps it was Kamalaya working its magic on me again. On

April 29, 2011, the day of the Royal Wedding, I was back in Ka-malaya. For several days I would rest, detox, and meditate in this nirvana, my every creature need met, my external world quiet and complete.

I was doing well, I thought. I helped my daughters get ready for the wedding by telephone, even trimming the feathers on Eugenie's hat over the airwaves. I gave Andrew a picture of me to carry in his pocket that day . . . and he did.

I awaited the onset of tranquility . . . but my melancholy would not cooperate. Rather than melt away, it bloomed all out of pro-portion. I missed the excitement and buzz of wedding fever, and, in particular, a Royal one. I said: "This can't be happening. You're the Duchess of York. You should be wearing a new designer suit, walking into the Abbey, taking a seat with your family, then shak-ing hands with the wedding party."

Sadness enfolded me; it obscured the happy sounds of nature and eclipsed the radiant sun through the palm trees.

Had I had the chance I would have inhaled food and binged to the highest peak of addiction. I wanted desperately to feed the gaping pain and hole in my heart. I fell headlong into my own melancholy—the regrets, the lost marriage, the lost dignity, the shame, all the things I would have done differently.

I canceled most of my appointments in Kamalaya and sat alone in my room and allowed myself to just be. I just lay there and felt the pain of the moment, and of the next one, and the next one. I didn't stiff-upper-lip myself. I stayed under the covers. I cried. I cried some more. I tried to feel as bad as humanly possible. Friends might have advised, "Pull yourself together, you're so lucky, you've got two girls, you've got your health." But I just let myself feel bad.

Then something within me began to shift: an internal changing of the guard, of the past relinquishing itself to the future—my future. I had broken into the sadness and I hugged my pain . . . and it wasn't so terrible after all.

Once you stop fighting the pain or trying to mask it, it loses its viselike grip over you. You have to embrace it; it lets you know there's life there. It is the bright light of hope and strength for healing. It gives you the wisdom and inner confidence to know that it's not the end of the world.

Unless we feel the pain, we can never get past the sadness or hurt.

I was moving forward, shedding a skin, realizing that the purpose of being human is to undergo metamorphosis.

On April 29, I said "good-bye" . . . good-bye to an old existence that I am no longer part of. I fully accepted that it is in the dark places that we find ourselves. My days had often been dark, and I knew the light would be wonderful when it came.

32 | *Found*

*I charted a course to serve me, and the wind
brought me home.*

$\mathcal{M}$Y JOURNEY CHANGED me in ways small and large. I am no longer the fixer of my parents' brokenness, nor the perfect princess or duchess who is expected to get it all right. I am not the person who used to beat herself up emotionally because she thought everything that went wrong was her fault. I am not the person who spends all of her time trying to win approval so everyone will like her.

That person has vanished, and there is no need to send out a search party.

In her place is simply Sarah, me at my true core.

I used to feel abandoned because, really, I abandoned myself. At age twelve, I locked up my true self, and I remember buying the padlocks. I created a person, someone I didn't want to be, who I hadn't been able to get in touch with for a long time. I felt totally and utterly useless. I had created quite a pity party for myself and it was a party of one. There were moments when I felt panic that maybe I was just a shell of a person, that there really was nothing left inside. I lost myself in that life for a long time.

Between my true self and where I stood, there fell a distance. And so I set out to transverse that gap and discover who I am, not so that my family or friends know but so that I would know. I questioned every part of my life, layer after layer, deeper and deeper.

The experience awakened my heart and connected me to the joy, love, and wisdom inside me. It enabled me to recognize and see angles and corners of myself that I neither knew about nor believed existed. I grew aware of possibilities and quantities of freedom that loosened the locks and chains that had gathered rust over so many years. I let my true self out of prison.

Slowly I learned to feel free and whole, whereas previously I'd let fear, anxiety, and anger gnaw at me and dictate my way of thinking and acting. I had acquired these destructive emotions from my environment and took them to be the most suitable armor for defending myself against a sea of pain, fear, and desperation.

Of everything I faced, the most testing thing of all was self-hatred. Before, when I looked in a mirror, I did not think nice things about myself. Or if I walked into a room, and someone looked me up and down, I would immediately think I had done something wrong, that I looked awful or ugly, or that that person didn't like me. I believed the hatred of myself to such a degree, that if horrible things were written about me, I believed them to be true.

I no longer think like that.

I discovered I am smart. I am special and unique. Very sensitive, loving, caring, and *sooo* funny. My friends and family will love me no matter what. I am important. I have the right to love and to be loved. I can be whatever I want to be, because I already possess all I need to succeed.

I discovered, too, that the best job I have ever done was as a mother. It has been my greatest joy to watch my daughters unfold—formulating their own beliefs and values from the foundation I created for them. I have simply watched them in this process, needing to step in very seldom. They live with the power of example, and I have taught them to find love in everyone, never shutting the door, even if that means only a small crack of life, love, or light can shine through.

Have you ever considered why, on an airplane, the flight attendant tells you to put on your own oxygen mask first, before you help your child? It is because your child's well-being depends on it. If you aren't grounded, present, calm, and able to breathe, there is no way you can help others. I have learned to put my own oxygen mask on first. If I don't nurture myself first, I'll have less nurturing to give to those who most need me.

I am living proof that patterns of unhealthy behavior as well as decades-old issues of self-hatred can—with intervention, examination, and commitment—be changed. In the sixth decade of my life, I look back on my times of turbulence, and, in a way, I am grateful they happened. If I had not taken the wrong path I would not be where I am today. Finding myself, and then getting myself back, are the true beginnings of a better life.

Are there aspects of myself I am still working on? Absolutely. I am working hard to forgive myself for my divorce and leaving Andrew. We had such a love, we still do, and although we now both love each other unconditionally, to live with regret is so difficult. Every day I face it. A very dear friend of mine says, "Forgiveness comes when you give up hope of being able to change the past." So true.

I still go back and forth about answering my critics. My conceived notions of others' opinions were so much a part of me and shaped my overall self-concept. As hard as I tried to ignore the cruel comments of others, they eventually became subconsciously embedded in my mind. Now I realize that, in one sense, acknowledging them gives them power. In another sense, defending yourself can be a source of strength. Either way, there is a fine line between getting into a useless name-calling game and trying to right the wrongs. Sometimes I think it seems pointless to try to counter the critics because they will always be there. But, honestly, I would like to live in a world where people are judged by what they actually do instead of what the media says they do.

I know I am a work in progress. I am sure to make mistakes. But I am no longer afraid of adversity. I can see it as the gift it really is. Adversity tests our courage, forces us to create new solutions, and imbues us with empathy for others and the world. When we face adversity, we can do one of two things. One, we can learn from the experience, strive to do better, apply ourselves, and rearrange our lives to make it work, and maybe pull it off, despite a rocky start. Or, two, we can receive the information of our failure as feedback, use it to help us learn about ourselves and figure out where we could best direct our energies. Adversity is our greatest teacher.

It taught me that our most important task is to conquer the demons that rob us of living full out every moment of every day.

Here is what I would ask of you: Examine your own life and truly take a look at yourself. Do you feel you have charted the course you desire? With the knowledge that our time on earth is limited, it is important that you ask yourself if you are living life well. Are you living with a sense of joy, happiness, and generosity to others? If not, what do you need to do to change your direction? Fortunately, this process of recognition, review, self-understanding, and insight can lead you to find the promise of peace, hope, love, and joy that exists in every one of us.

The essay "The Station" by Robert J. Hastings contains these wonderful lines:

> *But uppermost in our conscious minds is our final destination—for at a certain hour and on a given day, our train will finally pull into the station with bells ringing, flags waving, and bands playing. And once that day comes, so many wonderful dreams will come true. So restlessly, we pace the aisles and count the miles, peering ahead, waiting, waiting, waiting for the station.*
>
> *"Yes, when we reach the station, that will be it!" we promise ourselves. "When we're eighteen...win that promotion...put the last kid through college...buy that 450SL Mercedes-Benz...have a nest egg for retirement!"*
>
> *From that day on we will all live happily ever after.*
>
> *Sooner or later, however, we must realize there is no station in this life, no one earthly place to arrive at once and for all. The journey is the joy...*

So stop pacing the aisles and counting the miles. Instead, swim more rivers, climb more mountains, kiss more babies, count more stars. Laugh more and cry less. Go barefoot oftener. Eat more ice cream. Ride more merry-go-rounds. Watch more sunsets. Life must be lived as we go along. The station will come soon enough.

As for me, I am sitting in the sunlight and looking out over my bluebell wood. I do not know when I will arrive at the next station in life, or what it will bring, but in waiting for it, I feel more excitement than I do apprehension. I have purpose, I have joy, I have peace, I have love.

And I can see my smile in a cup of tea.

NUGGETS:

- Don't believe that everybody has the right to answer—check with yourself first.
- I want to tell you that no matter how insurmountable your problems may seem, you can change yourself for the better. If I can do it, so I can you.
- I'm living my life as I see fit, despite what others think or what the press say about me. Today I am living my life according to my truth.

S

Girlies we are the Tripod; we are united with our golden cord wrapped around our Hearts. Wherever, whenever, TOGETHER.

I am a work in progress, my new life is just beginning. It feels like I have just woken up from a long dream. I am now awake and aware, and it feels like a peaceful warm blanket to my heart and soul. I am honored to be your Mother, in fact it is the one job that I have done really well. I am never more proud of you in every way, you are strong, confident, hard working and true to the depths of your Hearts. No mother could beam with more pride and joy than when I look into your eyes and squash you into a Bear Hug of excitement when I see you.

I love you my Dearest Darling Angels.

your devoted

Mumsie xxx

Acknowledgments

TO ALL THE staff at Royal Lodge, led by Terence Holdforth. I thank you from the bottom of my heart for your goodness and for making it possible for me to stand and smile. To Amanda-Jane, my friend who has been by my side forever.

To Colin Tebbutt, Dafydd Jenkins, Harry Galliven, Phil Danvers, and Mark Harry—your loyalty knows no bounds. Thank you, Colin. We have seen each other through thick and thin, you have been constant to me and my family, and words are not enough to honor you. Thank you.

To all my devoted staff, past and present, who have stayed strong and robustly loyal at the coalface. Thank you all for never ever letting me fall, when I am sure you must have been weak with exhaustion.

To Madge—my dear Kate Waddington. You have been for twenty years at the coalface with me; I cannot thank you enough and always I send big love . . . And to all at Sputnik—thank you, especially Katherine.

To John-Boy, I will never forget you XX.

To Helen Jones—I miss you and your loyalty knows no bounds—with my devoted love.

To Gerry Casanova with love and thank you to my artistic Libran.

To Paul Lachman, thank you for your kindness and loyalty.

To my magical friends who have remained steadfast, kind, and full of compassion. I am so deeply grateful for your friendship—thank you.

To Poppina . . . your mother, Carolyn, my Angel, would be so proud of you, love you x.

To my Debonnaire and Eric Buterbaugh, you MADE it possible to carry on. All love and thank you.

To my darling Frooty, Christopher Ambler, and Poppy, you are my family and your strength is beyond words.

To Giuseppe Cipriani—you are always my shelter in a storm. Thank you.

To Stefania and Olivia Girombelli with love & LADY BUGS.

To my dearest Bonita, you are my lovely most special sister.

To my lovely darling Lee who makes my life shine, and everyday is better with her in it.

To Martino and Grant, you make my life better.

To Simon Griffiths and his lovely wife, Lisa, how do you manage with such compassion and love? Thank you for all my financial support.

To Amanda Thirsk, thank you for all your help. I am deeply grateful to you. You always keep calm and fight on for the family.

To Tim and Janey Ryan, thank you for your magical friendship—and for always being at the end of the telephone and for being there when my world fell apart.

To James Henderson, thank you for your unending patience

and loyalty in the press trenches. To Alex Boyd-Carpenter thank you for keeping James and me upright whilst looking after all my press and publicity.

To Amanda Lewis—with my love and here's to Khyber Road! Thank you.

To Camilla de Caires and your kind heart. Thank you.

To Rachel Virden, thank you for your enthusiastic goodness, and always picking up the telephone.

To Harry Keogh, Mark Simmons, and all at RBS. Thank you.

To Sachi Caldera at HSBC. Thank you.

To Marcus Leaver and all at Sterling Publishers.

To Josh Salzman, my buddy.

To Marcus Weston, you are my shining star.

To Karen Wellman and Zana Morris, thank you.

To all my charities, you give me the strength to go on. Thank you.

To Children in Crisis and my friends at Stewart's Road.

To Olivier and Zoe de Givenchy.

To Libby Caudwell—You are my shining star and I love my Libs.

To John and Claire Caudwell and your kind strength in adversity; when all turned their backs, you did not.

To S. With love and thanks from your Emma Harte.

To Hugh Lillingston, you have changed my life. Thank you.

To all the porters and doormen in the hotels that I visit. Thank you.

To all at Heathrow and Gatwick Special Services, you make my life so much easier.

To Mimi Poskett and Antonia Marshall with so much gratitude and big love.

To Heather McGregor, thank you for all your advice, friendship, and love.

To all my lovely friends at the OWN network.

To Lisa Erspamer, Kimi Culp, Rod Aissa—what would my life be like without you? Thank you so much.

To my Lisa (Louis and Lily). You have never broken your word, you are a pillar of strength, and you guide me with creative brilliance. Thank you, my sister.

To Kimi and her babies, thank you for fighting for me.

To Cindi Berger and Janet Ringwood, you are professional, strong, kind publicists, thank you.

To all my special friends at World of Wonder—thank you.

To Fenton Bailey, thank you for believing in me all those years ago.

To my lovely Elise Duran, you are my special friend lovely hairy dog.

To Anne Keating, with all my love and thank you.

To Ken Sunshine, my friend who suggested going to Oprah.

To Jack and Cindi Mori. Thank you for helping me to Oprah and being so kind and full of love.

To Heidi Krupp, thank you for helping me to Oprah with love and thanks to you.

To Dr. Peter Prociuk, for all your help, advice, and support. You have been amazing.

To Libby Moore and Peggy, and the Sarah Summit. You have held on to Sarah, and thank you for caring so deeply.

To my little magician lady, the beautiful Robin McGraw, with my love and so many thanks.

To Dr. Phil, thank you for all your friendship, wisdom, and being the giant of strength who has guided my life.

To Suze Orman, LYLAS. I have no words to thank you, I follow in your footsteps. Thank you for your loving guidance and goodness.

To KT, for kindness and love and mustard pots!

To Anamika, you are my shining star, my steadfast friend, my rock in stormy waters. I love you.

To Martha Beck, thank you for being incredible and my sister. All my love to you.

To Koelle, you are superb and so much love.

To Mark Nepo, you have inspired me, and thank you from my heart.

To Prudence Hall and all at the Hall Health and Longevity Center. You have given me my energy and life back. Thank you.

To my friends Ken Browning and Julie Groome, thank you.

To Eric and Mary Cowan, thank you so much for all your guidance and compassion and so much love.

To Bill and Aimee Beslow and all the magic of Charlotte and Beatrice. Thank you so and much love.

To Sara Weinstein, you give me strength, love, and wisdom. I admire you.

To Faith Cheltenham, you are exceptional and now you Twitter and connect me to the world—you live up to your name. Thank you.

To Nick Gonzales, with my huge thanks for your expertise and help.

To Agnes, my sweet Polish hairdresser, thank you.

To Tatyana, with all my thanks.

To Kat Miccio, with my huge thanks and love.

To John Scott, thank you so much.

To Larry Schwartz, you are my Planet.

To Angela Mathes Shapiro, with all my friendship, love, and thank you.

To Lou Palumbo and Kevin Jacobsen. I will never be able to thank you enough.

To Claudio Visconti, my fast and furious driver—thank you.

To Stedman Graham, thank you so much for all your wise and strong advice—you are a pillar of strength; I am in awe of your wisdom.

To Janet Ripley, thank you.

To Angella Cole and your deliciousness from Picky Eaters. Thank you.

To all the Affleck family. Thank you for my stay in Yellow-knife.

To Ray Zahab and Bob Cox. You make Impossible to Possible.

To Terry Woolf, I won't forget your words in the Arctic, they inspired me to carry on.

To all my friends in Spain and lovely Michele and Dave.

To Paula Wiseman, thank you for your kindness in always being there for me with love.

To Linda Medvene and Gabriella, you are always with me with love.

And finally to all those who have helped me with this book:

To Judith Curr, thank you for this amazing book and for your patience and friendship.

To Emily Bestler, for all your publishing brilliance.

To Kate Cetrulo, thank you for your hard work. So kind. Thank you.

To Kimberly Goldstein, wonderful support and kindness with this book. Thank you.

To Isolde Sauer, fantastic support and kindness with this book. Thank you.

To Jan Miller—thank you, my lovely. The best literary agent and dynamo.

To dearest Maggie Greenwood Robinson, your kindness and love and compassion in your own adversity is quite unequaled. Thank you so much for making such an extraordinary difference in my life and for making this book possible. You believe in me, when I don't or didn't. Thank you.

To Debbie Hare who sat for hours proofreading the manuscript until she became white with tiredness! With all my love and thank you so much. You are so creative and always here for me.

To Martin Huberty who also sat for hours proofreading the manuscript until he became white with tiredness! Also for your steadfastness; your loyalty is beyond words.

Photography Credits

Page iv: The photograph is by Brian Aris.

Page 7: The photograph is by Mike Erwin and is reprinted with the permission of the Great North Children's Hospital Teenage Cancer Trust.

Page 103: The photograph is by Brian Aris.

Page 113: The photograph is by Brian Aris.

Page 135: The photograph is by Robin Layton.

Page 211: The photograph is by Robin Layton.

Page 307: The photograph is by Robin Layton.

All other photographs are courtesy of the author.

Text Permissions

The author and publisher would like to thank the following sources for their kind permission to reproduce the materials cited below. Every effort has been made to obtain permission to quote from all third-party material, but we would be happy to correct any errors or omissions in future editions.

Page 45: The email from Marcus to the author contains a quote by Yehuda Berg. Used with permission of Yehuda Berg.

Pages 107–108: "When You Are Old" by William Butler Yeats, quoted from *The Collected Works of W. B. Yeats, Volume I: The Poems, Revised,* edited by Richard J. Finneran. New York: Scribner, 1997.

Page 141: "Grieve Not" by Mary Elizabeth Frye.

Page 151: John Daido Loori quote and the poem "The Path" are from *Perseverance* (2011), by Margaret J. Wheatley. Reprinted with permission from Berrett-Koehler Publishers.

Page 264: "Leisure" by William Davies. Used by permission of Kieron Griffin as Trustee of the Mrs. H M Davies Will Trust.

Page 299: "The Station" by Robert J. Hastings. Reprinted by permission of the Hastings Estate, © 1980.